AMERICA'S STATE FAIR IMPRESARIO

AMERICA'S STATE FAIR IMPRESARIO

The Life and Times of Mike Barnes

CORY FRANKLIN

Guilford, Connecticut

An imprint of The Rowman & Littlefield Publishing Group, Inc.
4501 Forbes Blvd., Ste. 200
Lanham, MD 20706
www.rowman.com

Distributed by NATIONAL BOOK NETWORK

British Library Cataloguing in Publication Information available

Library of Congress Control Number: 2019951691

ISBN 978-1-4930-5381-0 (cloth)
ISBN 978-1-4930-5383-4 (electronic)

♾™ The paper used in this publication meets the minimum requirements of American National Standard for Information Sciences—Permanence of Paper for Printed Library Materials, ANSI/NISO Z39.48-1992.

This is my father's story

It is a blessing to know your family's history

Mary Galvin

January 2, 2019

Contents

FOREWORD

NONE OF US HAS MORE THAN A FLEETING MEMORY, IF ANY MEMory at all, of our grandfather, Mike Barnes. He died nearly a lifetime ago, when we were very young or not yet born. Until now, most of what we knew about him came from anecdotes from our parents—his daughters and sons-in-law. They all described him as a model family man, a devoted husband and doting father.

One of the things that characterized Mike's life was his uncanny foresight. He could predict what was likely to succeed in business and in investing, and in the same fashion he always anticipated his family's needs. Fortunately for us, he was also meticulous in his business affairs and his private life. In this respect, he took precious care in his annotations, probably aware that his descendants would someday take the time to examine them. Not surprisingly, he was correct. He left a painstakingly curated scrapbook composed primarily of yellowing, decades-old newspaper articles from across the country that detailed his illustrious career. Along with this, we have photographs of his twin treasures: his work and his family.

From this scrapbook and these pictures, author Cory Franklin has been able to fill in many of the details and provide us with a rich picture of his amazing life. His book has whetted our appetites to learn more about this man, whose story stretches back nearly 150 years to the nineteenth century.

———

And what a remarkable story it is! Motherless at a very early age, Mike survived the hardscrabble streets of New York City, educating himself at the public library and in the newspaper trade. He rose above poverty and loss of family, and with virtually no formal education, he built a business that not only survived but thrived through the Great Depression. It is a tale as instructive as any found in the Harvard Business School Case Study Handbook. More than that, he found the great love of his life in his "Billie," our grandmother. He built a tight-knit family that is close today, in large part because of his efforts. Reason enough for us to read about him.

But this book is also a brief chronicle of what entertainment in America was like 100 years ago, an account that is woefully neglected in today's history books. At one time, county and state fairs provided the best, and in many places the only entertainment to be enjoyed, long before radio and television. While these fairs were quintessentially American, the entertainment included performers, attractions, and animals from all over the world, who dazzled the public and ensured great crowds at each fair. Most people today are unaware of the size and scope of state fairs in that era, and no one was more important in their development than Mike Barnes. He was truly a giant in that facet of twentieth century American life.

Dr. Cory Franklin has authored several books, and he has demonstrated that he is a mindful student of American history, especially that of Chicago. In this portrait, Dr. Franklin places our grandfather in the context of a rapidly changing century and a rapidly changing city. Along the way, we have brief encounters with movie stars, gangsters, corrupt politicians, and even the Beatles. It's a great read, and we're especially lucky to learn more about our grandfather, who left us his scrapbook and his legacy.

———

This book is dedicated to Mike's wife, Billie, and his two daughters: his surviving daughter, Mary, and her late sister, Betty Jane. We want to thank everyone in the Sheridan-Galvin family who participated in this project, and trust that this book will become a family heirloom. From the time Mike was born until today has been almost 150 years, and we fervently hope that our grandchildren and great-grandchildren will still be reading Mike's story well into the twenty-second century. With all that said, a special thanks to our parents who shared their stories about Mike Barnes, an exceptional man.

Pam Sheridan Pappano
Gail Galvin Ellis
Dawn Galvin Meiners
Christopher Galvin
Betsy Sheridan Collins
Michael Galvin
Philip Sheridan

CHAPTER ONE

Prologue

WHEN MIKE BARNES DIED IN 1956, THERE WAS AN OBITUARY written in the June 9 issue of *Billboard*, the entertainment industry magazine that had chronicled his achievements and successes for four decades. It described him thusly, "In the fair booking business, he was widely regarded as a man of integrity. He was generally given credit for having given stability to the booking field and also with having aided the development of the fair field through the introduction of revues and of many novelty acts."

His death was important enough to also merit an accompanying editorial that began, "There is no picture of Mike Barnes in this issue. By news standards, there would be. Mike . . . merited such treatment. There is no picture of Mike Barnes because of Mike's dying request that publications refrain from publishing one of him at his death. And we yield to that. He did not sell his personality, he sold his product. As the saying goes, he was all business." There are no obituaries of him on the internet. This is an especially telling fact about Mike Barnes—having a long career in show business, where promotion and public display are the coin of the realm, Mike was not one to promote himself.

By these accounts, and those of his family who remember him, Mike Barnes was an intensely private person. For someone who was at the top of his profession for nearly thirty years, and who was so accomplished in other areas, there is remarkably little known about his life. He kept virtually no first-person notes, and because he died nearly a lifetime ago, none of his contemporaries are still alive. Family and friends who remember him were, with rare exception, children when they knew him. This makes writing his story difficult—but not impossible.

From newspaper accounts, photographs, and some other documents, we can learn the when and where of his life, and in some cases those facts will provide the why's of his life. When we combine that with the major historical events of his time, this gives us an appreciation of what he did and more than a little admiration for his accomplishments as well. His story, as presented here, becomes not simply "The Mike Barnes Story" but "The Life and Times of Mike Barnes," and it takes part during a fascinating era of American history.

One last observation in that respect: Mike's obituary and the editorial in the 1956 *Billboard*, while extensive, were buried deep in the newspaper around page 50. This was hardly a measure of his importance to the industry; had he died 20 years before it would have been front page news. Rather, it was a measure of how the industry and indeed even *Billboard*, which was called *The Billboard* during Mike's heyday, had changed. Starting in 1894, it was a weekly with regular news about circuses, circus performers, and circus life. It then became the newspaper of record for fairs, carnivals, and review shows. But the front pages of the 1956 *Billboard* were filled with stories about mid-twentieth century entertainment: movies ("Movie Theater Now Playground for

Kids"), television ("Time-Life Buys Into Person-to-Person"), and music ("Decca Pacts Der Bingle to 3-Yr. Renewal"). Today, those headlines and references are as recondite as the ones about the fairs of the 1920s. But even in that 1950s *Billboard* world, the life and times of Mike Barnes were worthy of two mentions in what was then the industry Bible.

Michael Harry Barnes was born July 9, 1876, five days after the United States Centennial. The year he was born, the president, Ulysses S. Grant, had been the country's greatest general a decade before, a military hero who guided the nation through its worst conflict of the nineteenth century. When Mike died in 1956, the president, Dwight D. Eisenhower, had been the country's greatest general a decade before, a military hero who guided the nation through its worst conflict of the twentieth century. Despite this coincidence, there is probably no period in human history in which the world changed more than in the nearly eighty years of Mike Barnes's life. Someone who time-travelled from 1940 to 2020 would be surprised by many things—computers, international travel, the discovery of the human genome—but for the most part that person would recognize today's world. Someone transplanted from 1876 to 1956 would not have believed the changes in the world in four score years.

The America Mike was born into was only beginning to emerge as a truly united country, at least in terms of one's ability to travel from one coast to another. The First Transcontinental Railroad had just made its inaugural trip across the country, arriving in San Francisco 83 hours and 39 minutes after leaving New York City. A decade before, the same trip would have taken weeks to months, either overland by covered wagon or by ship sailing around South America.

Some things don't change over time. America at the time of Mike's birth was hardly a peaceful nation. Violence had subsided since the end of the Civil War in 1865, but it remained a violent country. Racial animus was prevalent, especially in the South, in what was known as The Reconstruction Era. Despite being emancipated by the Civil War, Southern blacks were being stripped of political power and voting rights. Economically, many were little better off than they had been under slavery. The Indian Wars were at their height, with a confederation of 5000 Arapaho, Cheyenne, and Sioux tribesmen annihilating the 300 men of the 7th Cavalry Regiment under Lieutenant Colonel George Armstrong Custer at the Battle of the Little Bighorn in Montana. Wild Bill Hickok was killed in Deadwood, South Dakota (when he was shot, he was holding aces and eights, which came to be known as the "dead man's hand.") The James-Younger Gang, a band of former Confederate desperadoes led by brothers Frank and Jesse James, and Cole Younger, left Missouri and headed north to Northfield, Minnesota, to pull off a daring, but what they assumed would be an easy bank heist ("The Great Northfield Minnesota Raid," the subject of several movies). The town was lying in wait for the outlaws, and most of the gang were either captured or killed.

Mark Twain published *The Adventures of Tom Sawyer*, and Twain, the most astute observer of America at the time, referred to the era as "The Gilded Age"—a society with an overlay of gold covering a baser metal. He was referring to the economic inequality of a time when great fortunes were created through advances in industry, transportation, and commerce, while the urban and rural poor often lived harsh, brutal lives of poverty.

Yet there were positive signs as America began its second hundred years. Alexander Graham Bell received a patent for his new invention, the telephone. It was believed to be one of the most valuable patents ever awarded. Three days later, he made the first call to his assistant (*"Mr. Watson, come here, I want to see you"*). Another brilliant inventor, Thomas Edison, received a patent for the mimeograph machine, one of many inventions he was working on that transformed the world. Edison's invention of the first practical light bulb would come two years later and would play a significant role in Mike Barnes's career, because fifty years hence Mike Barnes's contribution to outdoor lighting at state fairs would become one of his most significant accomplishments.

The inaugural season of professional baseball began with the first championship captured by the Chicago White Stockings of the National League, led by Cap Anson and Albert Spalding. (Despite their name, the White Stockings were actually the first incarnation of the Chicago Cubs. The team known today as the White Sox did not become a franchise for another twenty-five years.) The country was in the grips of the first great Depression, the result of The Panic of 1873, but there were signs the worst was over.

But in terms of everyday life, the America of Mike Barnes's birth was a completely different world than that in which he died. Perhaps most importantly, 1876 America was a rural country. Nearly half the country's citizens supported themselves and their families through agriculture. Three-quarters of the country's population lived outside urban areas. By 1956, those numbers had turned around so that nearly two-thirds of Americans lived in or near cities, and fewer than twenty percent were farmers. This demographic shift had profound implications for the country's politics, economics, culture, and among other things, Mike's future businesses.

Other than Winston Churchill, who was two years old, most of the figures who shaped the world of the first half of the twentieth century were not yet born in 1876. Franklin Delano Roosevelt, Joseph Stalin, Mao Zedong, Adolf Hitler, Dwight Eisenhower, Babe Ruth, Jackie Robinson, Charlie Chaplin, and Pablo Picasso were all born after 1876.

Public health was virtually unknown in 1876. For males, life expectancy was twenty five years longer in 1956 than it was in 1876; for females, it was nearly thirty years longer. In 1876, infectious diseases were epidemic; people died routinely of tuberculosis, cholera, diphtheria, and what would be considered trivial infections today. (In some respects, the close quarters of urban living rendered infectious diseases more common and more dangerous than they would be in the rural environment.) There were, of course, no antibiotics or vaccines; pasteurization of milk and water purification were in their infancy. Without refrigeration, food would typically spoil, leading to sickness and occasionally death. Surgery was more often lethal than lifesaving. Infant mortality was not even a measurable consideration in 1876, but it was probably twenty to fifty times higher than it was in 1956.

Alexander Graham Bell's patent notwithstanding, there were no telephones in 1876. The world at night was dark. Larger cities may have been illuminated by oil lamps or occasionally gas lamps (Baltimore was the first American city to be lit by gas in 1816) but Edison's light bulb to illuminate streets was several years off. Henry Ford's Model T was still thirty years in the future, and there was no radio, television, or motion pictures.

Mike Barnes (1876–1956)

But there were state and county fairs, and peoples' calendars were built around them. According to Derek Nelson, who wrote in the book *The American State Fair* (2004), "Even before automobiles, as long as a state fair was within a day's travel, people came by the thousands. Schools closed. Hordes of people crossed the countryside, some walking, others riding in carriages, spring wagons, and the 'one-hoss shay.' If a fair was near a large city that had a station, trains brought visitors from neighboring states. Today, many folks readily travel to distant places and vacation several times a year, but those luxuries are recent developments. Before the turn of the twentieth century, from the Midwestern prairies to the woods of the Northeast, the week spent at the state fair once a year was the only vacation that most people had. Because it took so long to travel anywhere by wagon or carriage, fairgoers had to plan months in advance."

America would change immensely from the last decades of the nineteenth century to the time following World War II. So would state fairs. And more than any single person, the man responsible for the change in the state fair over that time was Mike Barnes. He was a visionary and would become the premier impresario of the state fair—hiring the performers, and acting as talent scout, businessman, manager, promoter, and producer all in one. Mike was to the state fair what Flo Ziegfeld and Billy Rose were to Broadway, what Louis B. Mayer was to movies, and what Ed Sullivan was to television. Mike's ideas and hard work were instrumental to the development of the state fair in the twentieth century: an integral part of American culture and entertainment.

CHAPTER TWO

From Sing Sing to Five Points— Carrying the Banner

When Mary Galvin reminisced about her father, Mike Barnes, she recalled one story about when she decided to varnish the family cabin cruiser in Chicago's Montrose Harbor. Mary didn't realize boats with teakwood were generally not varnished, and when her father found out he reprimanded her, but not too sternly. "He loved my sister and me, but he always paid attention to the little things, and he wanted to teach us to do the same. We were entitled daughters but in a good way. We always had an eye toward charity. My father gave us nice things because he grew up so poor, and he never had nice things. He taught us to appreciate everything and everyone." Mary's story was simple, but it spoke volumes about her father.

To say that Mike Barnes grew up poor would be an understatement. His childhood was straight out of a Charles Dickens novel. Mike was born in Brooklyn in 1876, just over a decade after Robert E. Lee surrendered to Ulysses S. Grant at Appomattox. His father had come to America in 1872 although his eventual

Mary Galvin on the Barnes family cabin cruiser

fate is unknown, and his mother died when he was a young boy. An abusive stepmother, of whom little is known, raised him in Sing Sing—not the prison, but the village in Westchester County, north of New York City where the notorious prison was located. In the nineteenth century, the name of the village today known as Ossining was called Sing Sing, until it was renamed early in the twentieth century to avoid confusion with the local correctional facility. But Mike was long gone by the time the town was renamed.

(The prison is best known for its role in the 1938 movie *Angels With Dirty Faces*, starring Jimmy Cagney. Sing Sing was the first prison the French sociologist and political theorist Alexis de Toqueville visited when he came to America in 1831, before publishing his groundbreaking report *On the Penitentiary System in the United States and Its Application in France* with lawyer Gustave de Beaumont. The phrase "going up the river," which means going to prison, came from the practice of sending habitual or serious offenders from New York City jails thirty miles north, up the Hudson River to Sing Sing prison. Sing Sing basically separated hardened criminals from the run of the mill pickpockets, burglars, grifters, and common thieves. The term was eventually applied to anyone being sent to any prison.)

Growing up as a boy in Sing Sing was an apt metaphor for young Mike. Living with his stepmother was like living in prison, and he "broke out" when he was ten years old. He ran away and went "down the river" to New York City. In some respects, this was leaving the frying pan for the fire. With only a quarter in his pocket and one year of public schooling, he landed on the Lower East Side of Manhattan in the area that is today between Park Row and Chinatown. He slept in hallways, coal boxes, and anything that would provide shelter from the elements. Unfortunately, nothing would provide shelter from the squalid and violent environment.

Today, Manhattan's Lower East Side is gentrified, but when Mike arrived as a boy on his own, it was one of the poorest and most crime-ridden neighborhoods in America. In the 1880s, one-third of a million people were crammed into a single square mile of the Lower East Side, making it among the most densely populated places on earth. Cholera, yellow fever, typhus, and tuberculosis were endemic in the crowded tenements filled with newly arrived European immigrants. Infant mortality was staggering.

The section of the Lower East Side where young Mike lived was the infamous Five Points neighborhood, the most notorious area of which was Mulberry Bend. Murder, extortion, prostitution, and robbery were the practices of the day in the sleazy back alleys with colorful names like Bandit's Roost, Bottle Alley, and Ragpickers Row. Gangs such as the deadly Whyos roamed the streets at will, intimidating even the police.

The Whyos, an Irish gang that had its roots in smaller gangs formed before the Civil War, got their name from the bird calls they made to each other to identify themselves as members of the gang. One Whyo gang member named Piker Ryan, arrested in 1884, was found carrying a list of services offered by the gang, starting with "punching" ($1) and carrying through to "both eyes blacked" ($3), "nose and jaw broke" ($7), "(black) jacked out" ($15), "ear chewed off" ($15), "leg or arm broke" ($19), "shot in the leg" ($20), "stab" ($21.50), and ending with "Doing the Big Job" (AKA murder for $100 and up). Lawlessness was the order of the day in Five Points, where Mike was trying to survive as a young teenager.

At the same time, the legendary American newspaper reporter, social reformer, and photographer Jacob Riis was writing about the neighborhood in an attempt to bring reform to it. His 1890 book, *How the Other Half Lives* (1890), shocked the conscience of his readers with factual but horrific descriptions of the slums of the Lower East Side. The book was the impetus for the first significant New York legislation to curb poor conditions in tenement housing.

Jacob Riis: Three Urchins Huddling for Warmth in Window Well on NY's Lower East Side, 1889. COURTESY JAMES MAHER PHOTOGRAPHY

It was also the forerunner of muckraking journalism, which, through practitioners such as Ida Tarbell, Upton Sinclair, and Lincoln Steffens, became an important remedial feature of American urban life at the outset of the twentieth century. In addition to writing about the slums, Riis began using a flash lamp to photograph the squalid conditions. This was one of the first times flashbulb photography was used in an urban setting. A young Mike Barnes just might be in one of those historic photographs.

To avoid a life of crime, and likely an early death at the hands of the gangs, Mike got a job as a newspaper boy. He became, in the argot of the trade, a "newsie." In the late nineteenth century "newsies" or "newsboys" were the main distributors of newspaper afternoon editions to the general public in urban areas. Newsies in Manhattan earned around 30 cents a day, but to earn that money they had to work all day and late into the night. They were forced to sell every single newspaper because they could not return to the newspaper offices with unsold copies, otherwise they would have to pay for them.

(The 1992 Disney movie *Newsies* and 2012 Broadway musical of the same name provide somewhat sanitized accounts of the life of the newsie. The action takes place during the 1899 newsboy strike, approximately a decade after Mike's initial newsie experience. Because newspaper magnates William Randolph Hearst and Joseph Pulitzer had long exploited their child-labor force to distribute newspapers, there had been several less publicized newsboy strikes in the previous decade, so it is probable Mike had similar experiences with the labor unrest on the streets of the Lower East Side. Interestingly, one of the key musical numbers of both the movie and the play is called "Carrying the Banner." In later life, "carrying the banner" became one of Mike's favorite phrases. When he was a prosperous Chicago businessman, he would often ask people if they ever "carried the banner," meaning did they work hard, stand up for what they believed, and represent themselves with pride.)

Like Mike, many of the "newsies" were orphans. Competition was stiff, because there were hundreds, perhaps thousands, of orphans roaming the streets of Lower Manhattan. This competition, and the underdog status of these orphans, created many kids who were resourceful, audacious, plucky, and quick-witted. Mike undoubtedly picked up those characteristics on the streets. Without question, he "carried the banner."

CHAPTER THREE

Saved by the Doldrums?

EVEN WITH HIS NEWSIE JOB, MIKE WOULD HAVE FOUND IT DIFficult to avoid the rampant criminality of Mulberry Bend in the 1880s. While perhaps not even yet a teenager, Mike made what in retrospect seems an incredible decision: he signed on as a cabin boy on a freighter bound for Panama. It is not hard to see why he wanted to leave the squalor of the Lower East Side, but why Panama? No one will ever know, but the answer may lie in the current events of the day.

Between 1881 and 1889, the French launched an extraordinary project to build a sea-level canal in Panama. The project was directed by the legendary French administrator Ferdinand de Lesseps, who had masterminded the building of the Suez Canal in the 1860s. The Suez Canal had been a tremendous international success, and de Lesseps assured investors that building a canal in Panama would be easier than building one in Egypt.

Work began in 1881 and required huge expenditures of money, materiel, and manpower. The French company building the canal relied on subcontractors, as well as skilled and unskilled labor, primarily from Ireland, Scandinavia, and the United States.

It is not unreasonable to assume that to escape the gangs of New York, Mike boarded a freighter for Panama looking for work on the French Panama Canal project. He didn't find it—and it may have been the biggest break of his life that he didn't. Most people today do not realize that the renowned de Lesseps was not an engineer. His skill was in securing the essential political and financial backing and then organizing the necessary technical support for such a monumental undertaking. Moreover, he was nearly 75 years old when the digging started.

The Frenchman drastically underestimated the problems the project presented. It was much more complicated than digging the Suez Canal; both locales were impossibly hot but the humidity, diluvial rains and tropical diseases of Panama were factors the French didn't have to consider in the Egyptian desert. He managed the project at a distance from France and made a number of ill-fated decisions. After nine years and an expenditure of $287 million (equivalent to more than $8 billion in 2019), the French abandoned the project.

The failure was blamed on mismanagement and corruption. Once a national hero, de Lesseps was found guilty, along with his son, of mismanagement by a French court. They were both fined and sentenced to prison. An elderly man by then in his eighties, de Lesseps avoided jail but his son spent a year in prison on a related bribery charge. Eventually, the United States bought the rights to the canal (it initially balked at the price of purchase and planned to build a canal through Nicaragua). Learning from the French mistakes, the United States was able to complete the canal and it opened in 1914, thirty-three years after the initial French effort. Although Ferdinand de Lesseps did not live to see the Panama Canal completed, his son did—and saw his father's reputation restored as well.

As mentioned before, Mike never worked on the French Canal project of the 1880s. The freighter he boarded in New York was a three-masted schooner subject to the winds. The location of the Panama isthmus in Central America, between the Atlantic and Pacific Oceans, as well as its proximity to the Equator, make it subject to treacherous, unpredictable trade winds and the occasional doldrums. The doldrums are the lack of surface winds that can leave a ship motionless at sea for days or even weeks. (Today, the term "being in the doldrums" refers to a state of inactivity or listlessness.)

For three months, Mike's schooner was likely caught in the doldrums, unable to reach Panama. Provisions ran low, and the crew was forced to fish for food. Scurvy broke out on the ship, a result of vitamin C deficiency. ("Limey," the pejorative term for people from England, comes from the practice of sailors in the British Navy adding lemon or lime juice to their grog to prevent scurvy.) As soon as the ship landed in Panama, young Mike shipped back to Galveston, Texas, and then he hopped a New York-bound freighter, never to become part of the abortive Panama Canal project.

The doldrums may have saved Mike's life. As much as corruption and financial misconduct, the French Canal project failed because of tropical diseases, primarily the twin scourges of yellow fever and malaria, both of which were endemic in the fetid, mosquito-infested swamps of Panama. During the construction of the 1855 Panama Railway connecting the Atlantic and Pacific, over 12,000 workers died and the project had to be suspended frequently for lack of able-bodied workers. Things were no different a quarter century later when the French began the canal project. Eventually, they lost 22,000 workers, creating a chronic shortage of labor, which may have been why Mike set sail for Panama looking for work in the first place.

(When the United States took over the effort in 1904, it brought Colonel William Gorgas as the head of hospitals and sanitation. Gorgas instituted a remarkable mosquito eradication program, drained swamps and wetlands, developed screened sleeping quarters, and quarantined infected individuals. His work was one of the great public health accomplishments in history. Yet even with this remarkable work, the United States lost nearly 6,000 people in the ten years it took to build the canal.)

In a 2012 commencement address, historian David McCullough wrote of the American construction of the Panama Canal, "I have just returned from a cruise through the Panama Canal. I think often about why the French failed at Panama and why we succeeded. One of the reasons we succeeded is that we were gifted, we were attuned to adaptation, to doing what works, whereas they were trained to do everything in a certain way. We have a gift for improvisation. We improvise in jazz; we improvise in much of our architectural breakthroughs. Improvisation is one of our traits as a nation, as a people, because it was essential, it was necessary, because we were doing again and again and again what hadn't been done before.

Going through the Panama Canal, I couldn't help but think about all that I had read in my research on that story of what they endured to build that great path, how much they had to know and to learn, how many different kinds of talent it took to achieve that success, and what the Americans did under John

Dredging rock-Mindi.

MINDI.

French dredge of the Panama Canal c. 1885. COURTESY OF LINDA HALL LIBRARY

Stevens and George Goethals in the face of unexpected break-downs, landslides and floods. They built a canal that cost less than it was expected to cost, was finished before it was expected to be finished and is still running today exactly the same as it was in 1914 when it opened. They didn't, by present day standards for example, understand the chemistry of making concrete. But when we go and drill into those concrete locks now, we find the deterioration is practically nil and we don't know how they did it. That ingenious contrivance by the American engineers is a perfect expression of what engineering ought to be at its best—man's creations working with nature. The giant gates work because they're floating, they're hollow like airplane wings. The electric motors that open and close the gates use power which is generated by the spillway from the dam that creates the lake that bridges the isthmus. It's an extraordinary work of civilization. And we couldn't do it any better today, and in some ways we probably wouldn't do it as well."

In Panama, death was ubiquitous, and Mike might have been one of the unfortunate laborers to succumb to the ravages of mosquito-borne disease—assuming he avoided the oppressive heat and foul drinking water. He was soon on his way back to New York, perhaps unaware of how close he came to becoming one of the thousands of victims of *Aedes aegypti* (the mosquito responsible for yellow fever) or *Anopheles* (the malaria-carrying mosquito).

Chapter Four

Time to Make Three or Four Fortunes

In the classic 1948 film, *The Treasure of the Sierra Madre*, three gold prospectors played by Walter Huston, Tim Holt, and Humphrey Bogart strike it rich in the mountains of Mexico. On their trip back to civilization, Bogart is killed by bandits, and their gold dust disappears in the wind. Afterward, Huston and Holt commiserate about their futures. Huston is an old man, but a Mexican village has offered to make him their medicine man. The young Holt has no idea what he will do. Huston tells him, *"Oh, you're young yet. You've got plenty of time to make three or four fortunes for yourself."* That's essentially the story of Mike Barnes on his return to New York after the unsuccessful Panama venture.

When he returned to New York, Mike wisely decided not to return to the same neighborhood he left. He still settled on the Lower East Side, but moved to an area north of Five Points, known as Kleindeutschland or Little Germany. This German neighborhood was composed of cramped tenement apartments, but not nearly as cramped as those of Five Points. Certainly, the neighborhood was more stable.

After the Civil War, nearly 30 percent of the population of New York was German, making it the city with the third largest German population in the world, after Berlin and Vienna. Most of the Germans lived in Kleindeutschland; the Yorkville area in Uptown Manhattan around 86th Street, which most people today are familiar with as the German section of New York City, did not become the city's main German neighborhood until the years before World War I.

The German immigrants of Kleindeutschland tended to have more schooling than the Irish immigrants of Five Points, who were second-class citizens even in their home country of Ireland. This must have had a profound influence on Mike. Aware of his paucity of education, Mike decided to go to night school. He was self-educated and probably taught himself to read and write, but he honed those skills during the 1890s. (Judging by some of his notes and letters in his later years, his cursive penmanship was beautiful.)

During the day, he resumed his job as a newsie (so he actually may have been involved in the notorious 1899 newsboy strike), and he eventually saved enough money to get a job as a messenger boy on Wall Street. While he was improving his reading and writing skills at night school, on Wall Street, and the surrounding open markets, Mike was learning the ins and outs of buying, selling, and investing. This education would prove invaluable and shape the rest of his career.

Mike soon graduated from being a newsie selling newspapers to actually working for them. His first newspaper job was as a printer's devil (an apprentice at the newspaper who does menial jobs like fetching type and mixing vats of ink) at a German newspaper, most probably *The New Yorker Staats-Zeitung und Herald*, the most prestigious newspaper in Little Germany. At the turn of the century, it had the third largest circulation of any newspaper in New York City, exceeded only by that of the *New York World* and *New York Tribune*. (*The New Yorker Staats-Zeitung* continues to

New York World Building 1905

publish today as a weekly.) With his experience, he became a copy boy at *The New York Journal*, then a reviewer for the new Jewish newspaper, *The Jewish Daily Forward*, and finally a reporter at *The New York World*. Mike always maintained that his newspaper work was the best education he ever received.

At the turn of the twentieth century, *The New York World* was one of America's leading newspapers, owned by Joseph Pulitzer and operating out of what was then the tallest office building in the world. Mike covered the Jefferson Market Court in Downtown Manhattan, which was located in the entertainment district, where he got his first exposure to show business. The courthouse was notable as the site of the first night court in America, as well as for a number of famous trials, including the first "Trial of the Century": the murder of architect Stanford White by millionaire Harry Thaw over the affections of chorus girl Evelyn Nesbit. (That infamous incident became the subject of E. L. Doctorow's novel *Ragtime*, which was turned into a Tony-winning Broadway musical and a popular movie starring Jimmy Cagney in his last feature film.)

After working at *The New York World* as a reporter, Mike was transferred to the circulation department, gradually working his way up to become chief of city delivery, where he made a number of business contacts. One night, while supervising the night delivery of newspapers to the Bronx, at a beer hall he ran into the paper's night club reporter, who had overindulged and was in no condition to write his night club column. Mike wrote the column for him so well that the reporter, more concerned with drink than deadlines, invited him to write it any time he pleased.

Mike soon made acquaintance with many music hall, beer garden, and vaudeville performers, who were anxious to employ the serious young man as their agent. He quickly realized that commissions for theatrical booking would be more lucrative than the newspaper business. While he was not fully committed to show business yet, he did once book the vaudeville team of Weber and Fields into a Hoboken beer garden.

(Weber and Fields went on to become one of the country's most popular comedy teams at the turn of the century. The 1972 play and 1976 movie, *The Sunshine Boys*, was inspired by either the team of Weber and Fields or the team of Edward Gallagher and Al Shean. When Weber and Fields split up, Lew Fields became one of the country's top theatrical producers. The most famous member of the family, however, was his daughter Dorothy. Dorothy Fields was arguably the most successful female lyricist and librettist in American history. Her songs included "On the Sunny Side of the Street," "The Way You Look Tonight," "A Fine Romance," "I'm In the Mood For Love," "Pick Yourself Up," "Big Spender," and "If My Friends Could See Me Now." Her musicals included "Annie Get Your Gun," "Sweet Charity," and "Sugar Babies." In 1971, she became the first woman to be inducted into the Songwriters Hall of Fame.)

One of his bosses advised Mike to save ten percent of his salary, and he subsequently put away an even greater fraction. He then took his first financial gamble—real estate speculation. By financing apartment houses in Brooklyn and Manhattan, he made his first fortune, albeit a small one. Then came the Knickerbocker Crisis, the Financial Panic of 1907.

In October of 1907, speculators tried, and failed, to corner the copper market. The futile effort by those speculators and their banking associates resulted in an immediate run on several smaller New York banks and trust companies. At the time,

Financial Panic of 1907 on Wall Street

trust companies were less strictly regulated than national or state banks. Even as the banks stabilized, the trust companies continued to fail. In less than two weeks, the Knickerbocker Trust Company, New York City's third-largest trust, could not withstand the run and failed. This triggered a generalized panic throughout the financial industry by the end of the month. The combination of shrinking market liquidity and lack of investor confidence placed New York City at the threshold of insolvency.

This parlous situation was saved by the financial giants J.P. Morgan and John D. Rockefeller. Morgan, especially, convinced bank presidents to provide money to prevent the New York Stock

Exchange from closing. Returning from vacation, he injected $30 million into the system by himself, through the purchase of city bonds. This brought liquidity and confidence back into the system, and the run on banks and trusts eventually stopped, even though the Dow Jones Index did not recover its previous highs for nearly four years.

Morgan and Rockefeller were hailed as heroes by some, but others felt the Panic of 1907 was an indication that too much power lay in the hands of a small group of financial titans. There was a widespread belief that the Federal Government could have prevented the situation by providing liquidity for distressed institutions through a central bank. All the major financial powers in Europe had central banks that could respond to conditions such as those that developed in October 1907 in the United States.

The most important consequence of the crisis was the creation of the Federal Reserve System, essentially the central bank of the United States. Leading financiers drafted a framework of monetary policy and reform for the banking system. However, it was not until December of 1913 that President Woodrow Wilson signed legislation creating the Federal Reserve System. Ironically, The Fed faced its first test less than a year later with the outbreak of World War I. By the end of the war in 1918, the Federal Reserve was one of the world's most important financial institutions.

Meanwhile, the Panic of 1907 busted Mike Barnes. He was broke—but not for long. And in fact, his experience with the Panic helped him immeasurably when another October, twenty-two years later in 1929, brought an even worse market crash. By then he would be a prosperous businessman, but after the 1907 experience, he first had to recover.

CHAPTER FIVE

A Gift For Reading The Market

MIKE'S FORTUNES WERE AT A LOW EBB AFTER THE 1907 PANIC.
He moved on from *The New York World*, which was undergoing
turmoil in its circulation wars with William Randolph Hearst's
New York Journal-American (Joseph Pulitzer and Hearst were
fierce rivals and some of this circulation battle was the model for
the early sequences in Orson Welles's 1941 classic film, *Citizen
Kane*). In addition, Joseph Pulitzer's poor health created more
instability at the newspaper at the time. For whatever reason,
Mike took a job as a salesman for a cigar company. Considering
the location, he may have worked for Barclay Rex, a venerable
tobacco shop near Wall Street that was opened by an Italian
immigrant in 1910 and remains open today.

Most likely, his intent by working as a salesman was to
acquire a working stake to pursue his interest in investing. When
Mike built his stake up to $50, he was ready to take a chance; he
decided to speculate in cotton. In 1910, there were two exchanges
in the United States where cotton futures were officially traded,
one in New York, NYCE (the New York Cotton Exchange,
the other in New Orleans, NOCE (the New Orleans Cotton

NEW YORK STOCK EXCHANGE C. 1907

Exchange). Typically, speculators in New York were bears, trying to drive down prices by shorting the market, while speculators in New Orleans were bulls, attempting to drive the prices higher. (New York was the home of The Garment District, and merchants there naturally wanted lower prices for cotton. New Orleans was in the South, where cotton was grown and picked, and local growers there obviously wanted higher prices.)

The situation between the two markets often drew the attention of regulators, but whatever the dynamic, Mike read it well and turned his $50 into $11,000. In 2019 dollars that $11,000 would be the equivalent of $300,000. In only two years, he had gone from near destitution to acquiring a small fortune. Mike truly had a gift for reading the market.

Years later during the Depression, when Mike was the top state fair impresario in the country, this gift for reading the market would save many state fairs. At the height of the Depression, many Midwestern state fair operators, who were farmers, did not want to risk putting significant money into fair attractions with corn prices sometimes dropping as low as ten cents per bushel. Mike had confidence, and more importantly, he could impart his confidence to farmers who were reluctant to gamble.

One year, in Muscatine County, Iowa, Mike went in to sell a show budgeted at $1200, a significant sum during the Depression. Fair members understandably balked, afraid the fair would not recoup the costs. Mike asked them what corn was selling at (of course he knew the answer before asking), and they replied thirty cents per bushel. When he asked them if they were willing to sell their corn at that price, they replied that they would wait, hoping the price would rise.

Mike agreed with that assessment. He told them, "As a matter of fact, I think the price of corn will hit fifty cents by the time the fair opens. I'm so sure of that, I will make a deal with you. I will supply the show in return for $1000 worth of corn at fifty cents per bushel at fair time." The fair operators were stunned by Mike's confidence, but they realized he was a savvy investor. Their confidence bolstered, instead of accepting Mike's proposition in terms of corn, they made an outright cash contract with him. Mike's prescience was proven once again: when the fair began, corn surpassed fifty cents per bushel and went to seventy-five. Not only during the Depression, but again in World War II, he reassured balky state fair operators and kept fairs in business. At the same time, he was able to guarantee work for acts whose finances were stretched during hard times.

He never lost his interest in real estate and commodities. At one time, he owned a seat on The New York Stock Exchange, and he was a long-time member of The Chicago Board of Trade. Not bad for someone who was essentially wiped out in the Panic of 1907. But he made mistakes as well, perhaps none as bad as his first investment upon moving to Chicago.

Chapter Six

A Business Failure and Blistered Feet in the Windy City

THROUGHOUT HIS LIFE, MIKE OPERATED BY TWO BUSINESS principles. One was that "if you are familiar with a business, back your judgment to the maximum and commit all the brains and money you have available to make it succeed." The other was a saying that he would often use when people came to him for advice, "never monkey with a business proposition you know nothing about." Unfortunately, or perhaps in the long run fortunately for him, that second piece of advice he dispensed was something he learned the hard way.

Flush with money from his cotton investments, Mike was persuaded in 1911 to come to Chicago by his older brother, Fred. Frederick Milton Barnes was born in Germany on September 2, 1870, five and a half years before Mike. Their parents were Austrian, but Austria had been defeated by the Prussian state in the 1866 Seven Weeks' War. This victory solidified Prussian dominance over the other German states and was the prelude to the 1871 Franco-Prussian War. The Austrian defeat would prove to be the beginning of the end of the Austro-Hungarian Empire, but the glorious empire would carry on in a weakened state until World War I (World War I itself was a consequence of the ongoing enmity between France and Germany after the Franco-Prussian War).

Meanwhile in the aftermath of the Seven Weeks' War, Fred's father, Herman, the family patriarch, moved the family from Austria to Germany, where Fred was born. (In a 1917 edition of *The Billboard*, in an alphabetical list of Members of National Vaudeville Artists, Inc., right below the name Fred Barnes there is the name Herman Barnes. It is not clear whether this is Mike and Fred's father.) A year later in 1872, after the Franco-Prussian War, the family emigrated to the United States. Mike was born at Kings County Hospital in Brooklyn four years later. He was the first Barnes born in America.

While Mike was growing up in New York City, Fred came to Chicago sometime around the turn of the century and moved to the North Side of the city, where many German immigrants lived. Those who didn't know the two would have never figured them for brothers. Mike was physically slight, taciturn, and didn't like to draw attention to himself. Fred was a large man with a touch of flamboyance about him. Mike was single, while Fred was

Fred Barnes

Purple Pierce-Arrow owned by Fatty Arbuckle

divorced with a young daughter. Mike didn't smoke (he did chew on matchsticks when he was nervous), while Fred smoked huge cigars and rode around in a massive, chauffeured Pierce-Arrow.

(The Pierce-Arrow was once one of the most prestigious names in the automobile industry, one of America's first luxury cars. Between 1901 and 1938, the Pierce-Arrow Motor Car Company in Buffalo, New York, produced some of the highest quality automobiles in the world. For three decades, Pierce-Arrows were common sights anywhere the rich and powerful could be found. William Howard Taft ordered two for the White House in 1909, and after that the company routinely supplied cars to the White House for state occasions. It became the first official presidential car, as well as the favorite car of corporate tycoons and business magnates. The company also sold cars to the royal families of Japan, Persia, Saudi Arabia, Greece, and Belgium. Disgraced silent film comedy star Roscoe "Fatty" Arbuckle was forever linked with his 1919 Pierce-Arrow Model 66 A-4 Tourer,

35

sprayed in a bright purple hue. Babe Ruth drove a Pierce-Arrow, as did Charlie Chaplin and Ginger Rogers. The car was priced as high as $10,000 during the Depression. However, without a low cost alternative to generate cash flow, the Pierce-Arrow Motor Car Company was forced into bankruptcy in 1938.)

Fred Barnes was an established fair booker in the Midwest when he returned to New York and urged Mike to join him in Chicago. Mike hesitated; he anticipated repeating his involvement in the type of real estate investments he had been successful with before the Panic of 1907. But he decided to take the plunge, because Chicago offered so many opportunities in real estate in the years before World War I. Chicago was "The City of Big Shoulders."

After the Chicago Fire in 1871, the population of Chicago grew rapidly. By the time Mike came in 1911, it had grown to 2.2 million, and then the city's population grew by more than 50 percent over the next two decades, approaching 3.4 million by 1930. Much of this growth came from migration, especially the African-American migration from the South and from foreign immigration from Southern and Eastern Europe.

Being the railroad hub of the country, Chicago was a manufacturing capital and a leading producer of many goods including furniture, tobacco, apparel, and candy. It was, of course, "The Hog Butcher to the World"—a name that came from the 1914 poem "Chicago" by Carl Sandburg:

Hog Butcher for the World,
Tool Maker, Stacker of Wheat,
Player with Railroads and the Nation's Freight Handler;
Stormy, husky, brawling,
City of the Big Shoulders.

Chicago in the 1920s

(Chicago's other familiar nickname, "The Windy City," is often thought to come from the winds coming off Lake Michigan that cool the city in the summer but are often bone-chilling in the dead of winter, or from the frequent spring thunderstorms that often buffet the region, spawning tornadoes. However, an alternative theory is that the name derives from the bluster of the local politicians. This nomenclature issue has never been settled.)

When Mike Barnes came to Chicago, it was certainly filled with corrupt and bombastic politicians. Less than five years after Mike arrived, the city elected its last Republican mayor, "Big Bill" Thompson. A swaggering Irishman with an animus toward the English, Thompson once promised voters he'd "crack King George one in the snoot" if the King ever set foot in Chicago.

Thompson was also known for his relaxed attitude toward the gangster element in Chicago. He served two nonconsecutive terms, eventually being defeated by Anton Cermak, who served only part of his elected term. (Cermak was killed by an assassin whose target was actually President-elect Franklin D. Roosevelt.) Meanwhile, Bill Thompson ran unsuccessfully for a number of offices and died alone in 1944. After his death, his safe deposit boxes were opened and found to contain $1.84 million in cash and securities.

Along with the corrupt political machine, organized crime was taking hold in Chicago. By coincidence, around the time Mike came out to Chicago from New York, another New Yorker was making the same trip west. Like Mike, Johnny Torrio was a veteran of the most violent part of the Five Points neighborhood, an up-and-coming young man, short, not ostentatious, with a

Johnny Torrio

quiet nature and a keen business sense. Neither man smoked, drank to excess, or cursed. Also like Mike, with his brother Fred, Johnny Torrio had a family connection in Chicago—his uncle was "Big Jim" Colosimo, a brothel owner looking to expand his criminal empire in Chicago. Both Mike and Johnny would have been successful in any business they went into, but that's where the similarities between Johnny Torrio and Mike Barnes ended: Mike was legit all the way, while Johnny was a gangster.

Once Torrio became comfortable in Chicago, he helped Colosimo become the top gangster in the city. With a quiet detachment, Torrio eliminated most of the threats to Colosimo's business, and extended his vice and gambling empire into the suburbs, a heretofore unprecedented expansion. Eventually, however, things turned sour between "Big Jim" and Torrio. Torrio was not happy with Colosimo's seeming lack of interest in the business, especially after Colosimo hesitated to go into bootlegging when Prohibition became the law of the land in 1919. Things became even more tense when Colosimo divorced Torrio's aunt to marry a showgirl.

One afternoon in 1920, Torrio asked Colosimo to meet him at a restaurant. An hour later, Colosimo was shot in the back of the head and killed. Colosimo's death was the first gangland killing of a major figure in Chicago. It would soon be followed by many more. It also marked the first extravagant gangster funeral held in Chicago. The most telling thing about the funeral was the number of prominent citizens and public figures who came to mourn. The massive crowd was filled with judges, politicians, madames and police brass, all there to pay respects to the city's top mobster.

Big Jim Colosimo's funeral

Big Jim Colosimo's killer was never apprehended. Some suspected it was a professional hitman from New York. Others suspected it was the young protégé who Johnny Torrio summoned from Brooklyn to help him oversee the bootlegging enterprise. Several years later, when the business became too violent for Johnny Torrio, he retired and turned over the entire Colosimo operation he had assembled to that protege. The young man's name was Al Capone.

While politicians and mobsters were gradually amassing illicit fortunes in the second decade of twentieth-century Chicago, Mike Barnes was out to make a legitimate fortune. Ironically, Mike's first attempt was not in real estate, nor was it in fair booking. Mike's brother Fred persuaded him to run a carnival. Fred was friends with two brothers, Charlie and Eddie Marsh, who described the amazing profits that came with owning a carnival. Being new to the city, Mike had no reason to doubt the Marsh Brothers, so he put up most of his cotton investment money to buy a carnival that consisted of rides, a Russian dance troupe, and a pit show (a show in which the attraction is displayed in a pit). The pit was usually not an actual hole in the ground but might be an area of the tent sectioned off by a canvas divider or a ground-level area viewed from above through a raised walkway). The carnival turned out to be an unmitigated disaster.

Reporter Herb Dotten told the story of Mike's abortive carnival venture in *The Billboard Magazine*. (Since the 1960s, *Billboard Magazine* has been primarily a magazine about different genres of music. Before that, it was an all-purpose entertainment magazine, known as *The Billboard Magazine*, and before that it was primarily about circuses.) This is Dotten's account as told to him by Mike:

> *After investing in his carnival, "Mike came to the realization that he didn't know anything about the carnival business. This alarmed him. He decided to find out about carnival operations. Hiding his identity, he roamed the midway of the Parker Shows, then owned by Con. T. Kennedy, mingled with the workers, asked questions and gathered information. And the information Mike recalls, was enough to assure him the carnival business was not for him.*
>
> *Returning to Chicago he made his stand plain. There were demurrers from the Marsh Brothers, not to mention brother Fred, who had signed up a Russian dance troupe for $150 per show. Rather than leave his brother in the hole, Mike declared he would take out the Russian troupe—but*

Mike Barnes c. 1915

nothing else—with a carnival. This he did, but he didn't stay out long.

The Russian dance unit opened with the Parker Shows at Ottawa, Kansas. By this time, Mike had put out $3,000 in make-ready, and the first night (a July 3rd) it took in $14.50. Mike had figured it would gross over $1000 over the Fourth. Instead, it got $128 after 11 shows. And the Russians got big blisters on their feet.

After the 11th show, the Russians struck. They protested their blisters wouldn't let them continue. Mike mulled that over and said, "I'm a greenhorn at this business. I have a contract for 29 more weeks. I'll tell you what I'll do. I'll give you a bill of sale for everything on the show and pay you the week's salary, and you can continue the show.

The Russians countered with, "No, you don't have to do that. Merely pay our fare back to Chicago, and we'll call everything off."

And that was how Mike closed his operation with a carnival."

Years later, Mike summarized his carnival setback philosophically, "I took my lickin' in the carnival business and got out."

CHAPTER SEVEN

Bouncing Back

MIKE WAS NEARLY BROKE AS A RESULT OF THE CARNIVAL DEBA-
cle, just as he had been after the Panic of 1907. But the grit,
determination, and resourcefulness he had learned on the streets
of New York and sailing on the Panama freighter would serve
him well in Chicago. He decided to return to his show business
roots and book vaudeville acts, recalling his experience in the
Bronx with the bibulous beer hall reporter. Ironically, it was the
Marsh brothers, in part responsible for his carnival failure with
their bad advice, who set him on his new path.

When Mike returned to Chicago after closing the carnival,
Charlie and Eddie Marsh had just closed a deal with a fiddle
player who was looking to change jobs. The Marshes offered
to teach the fiddle player how to enter the booking business in
exchange for a payment of $500. But the fiddle player wasn't cut
out to be a booking agent and when Mike heard about the situation, he gladly put up the $500, some of his last money, to refund
to the fiddle player and take his place. That was his entry into the
booking business in Chicago.

In terms of entering vaudeville when it was a thriving business, Mike's timing was not optimal. It had been the most popular form of entertainment in the country from roughly 1880 to 1910. While that scene was still quite active when Mike became involved and spawned many familiar performers for decades to come, the new medium of motion pictures would eventually presage the end of vaudeville. By 1930, for all practical purposes, vaudeville was on its last legs. The tinsel of Hollywood would be the shroud for the dying entertainment form. Ultimately, only the cheap burlesque houses would remain, and those too gradually died out by the 1960s.

Nevertheless in 1915, the number of vaudeville stops in Chicago was second only to that of New York. The largest vaudeville theaters in downtown Chicago seated 2,000 patrons. A couple of dozen smaller vaudeville theaters were located all over the city and larger outlying suburbs. An African-American owned-and-operated vaudeville house was located on South State Street. With all these theaters, there was a constant demand for performers, even after West Siders Barney and A. J. Balaban and Sam Katz opened the Chicago Theater in 1921, featuring movies and live entertainment for the same price as vaudeville-only shows. This was the beginning of the death of vaudeville in Chicago, but by then Mike was savvy enough to have moved into other enterprises.

(The ornate Chicago Theater, once the flagship of the Balaban and Katz Theater empire, still stands at 175 North State Street. Ownership has changed hands several times, but the theater still features live entertainment and movies. The distinctive theater marquee has been featured in countless movies and television shows, and is one of the most identifiable landmarks in the city. The building was added to the National Register of Historic

Chicago Theater 1927

Places in 1979, and its history is detailed in the book *The Chicago Movie Palaces of Balaban and Katz*, by David Balaban, grandson of the original owner.)

With his past experience and business savvy, Mike would soon become one of Chicago's biggest "10-percenters"—independent theatrical agents or brokers who took 10 percent of the fee a performer earned. (In the 1990s, there was a popular sitcom in Great Britain called the *10 Percenters*, set in a London theatrical agency.) A talent agency is sometimes called a "tenpercentery." Mike had once again returned from the brink of financial disaster, and he would never be in a financial hole again.

Mike may have seen the writing on the wall for vaudeville early on. The threat the movies presented might have occurred to him because in the middle of the 1910s, Chicago, not Hollywood, was the center of the movie industry. Mike was no doubt aware of the Chicago-based trade magazine *Show World*, which proclaimed that "Chicago leads the world in the rental of moving picture films and in the general patronage of the motion view." The first slapstick comedy to feature a pie fight, the first *Wizard of Oz* film, and the first feature-length Sherlock Holmes film were all filmed in Chicago. One of the prominent Chicago studios,

Charlie Chaplin in Chicago 1915

Essanay (named for the initials of its founders George Spoor and Gilbert Anderson) was the early home to both a young Charlie Chaplin and a teenage Gloria Swanson. It is tempting to imagine that Mike, in the entertainment business, met the two cinema legends during their brief time in Chicago.

By 1920, in search of better weather and a more liberal tax status, most of the film business had moved to Southern California. The realization that movies were the future and vaudeville was the past was probably not lost on the shrewd Mike Barnes. While booking talent for vaudeville was lucrative, he had his eye on something else—fair booking.

CHAPTER EIGHT

Taking Off At Riverview

WHETHER IT WAS BECAUSE MIKE SAW THE DEMISE OF VAUDE-
ville coming in the wake of the movies or whether it was because
his brother convinced him that fair booking was where their
future lay, the economics stood clearly in favor of going into fair
booking over being a 10-percenter. Rather than charging on a
commission basis, fair bookers worked on an "over and above"
basis. If an act charged $250 for a week's work, a 10-percenter
got $25 of the money. Fair bookers could take the same act and
sell it for as high a price as they could negotiate, and then keep
everything over the base $250. There was little question that fair
booking was the more lucrative venture.

Each fair booking agency had a number of circus or novelty
acts signed up for the fair season, usually from about May 15th
to October 15th (the Texas fair season usually ran a week longer
than the others). The acts were guaranteed a certain minimum
number of weeks work, most contracts specifying at least eight
or ten weeks to be played within the three-month period. Each
agency would attempt to peddle the greatest number of its own
acts to the most fairs possible, for the largest price obtainable.

The agency would sign up a man and woman aerial team at a salary ranging from $175 to $250 per week, and then sell the act to the fair for every possible dollar above these figures. An act signed up with a Chicago booking agency for $200 a week would frequently sell to the fair for $400. In the above instance the fair secretary, at the conclusion of the fair, paid the act its presumed salary of $400. The act retained its own $200 (its actual negotiated salary with the booking agency) and forwarded the remaining $200 to the Chicago booking agency—a profit of 100 percent rather than the usual 10 percent (the agency made $200 rather than the $20 a 10-percenter made.)

It was customary for a county fair association to hold a meeting in January or February of each year, at which time they voted appropriations for their fair, which would be held the following autumn. As an example, the fair might vote $10,000 for races, premiums, and free attractions. The $10,000 would perhaps be distributed as follows: $3000 as purses for the harness races; $2000 to be cut up into a number of prizes for the best corn, cows, beans, bulls, lettuce, lambs, and other agricultural products of the county; and $5000 for "free attractions" i.e., the acrobatic, aerial, and animal acts that performed between races on a platform in front of the grandstand. This free attraction money was the grand prize for which the Chicago fair booking agencies competed furiously. Mike and the agency would earn their cut from the money the fair association set aside for their acts, from corporate sponsorships and advertising in newspapers and fair bills, and from the admission fairgoers were charged. Some fairs, like the Topeka Free Fair, could put on their fairs without charging admission. The fair agency booking acts would still make their money from the appropriation set asides and the corporate contributions.

The financial transactions involved in the fair booking game must have reached impressive totals during the "good" years. Consider, for example, Iowa with its ninety-nine counties, each one of them running an annual county fair. In addition, there were always a vast number of State Fairs, Tri-State Fairs, Fall Festivals, etc. During the prosperous years during the Roaring Twenties, the Illinois State Fair, held annually at Springfield, frequently spent $25,000 for free attractions for a single week.

Mike had enough of a stake from his time as a vaudeville agent to join brother Fred as a fair booker. He reasoned that his experience in evaluating talent would transfer well to bringing variety acts to the big state fairs across the country. To begin with, the two brothers decided to promote singing, dancing, and variety acts as grandstand attractions.

Mike recalled, "The fair managers used to call them 'free acts'. They did that because people could get up on high places on the fairgrounds and see the acts even though people were paying to get into the grandstand to see them." But Mike had the foresight to realize that in the long run those shows would be good entertainment for crowds and profitable for everyone.

(Many years later, when interviewed by *The Kansas City Star*, Mike talked about the scale of the business. He said of the years when he booked ten of the largest state fairs in the Midwest, "I can tell you that those ten fairs spend in excess of $500,000 for their grandstand night attractions. Of course, the admission take runs much higher than that. This is really a multi-million dollar business." Today, that would translate into hundreds of millions of dollars, a little-heralded but huge industry.)

In 1918, the Barnes brothers first tried out their variety act review locally in Chicago. They auditioned singers, dancers, and bands for their "experiment." Mike said, "I remember we called it the 'League of Nations' review. The thing that made it was the fact that we had lots of dancing girls, music, and lots of swirl. We had spectacle numbers with a lot of flags from various countries."

(The League of Nations was the forerunner of the United Nations, an international diplomatic group whose charge was to prevent warfare by solving disputes between countries. It was first convened in 1919 after World War I, but before that, in 1918, when the Barnes brothers named their review for it, the League of Nations was an important point of discussion in the United States. In January of 1918, President Woodrow Wilson gave his famous Fourteen Points speech, where he presented a comprehensive program designed to maintain world peace after the horrific slaughter of World War I, which was winding down and would eventually end later that year. The League of Nations was part of Wilson's overall proposal.

As it turned out, the Barnes brothers were overly optimistic with the name of their review, because the United States never wound up joining the League of Nations. There was vigorous debate across the country regarding Wilson's proposal during 1918, and after the Treaty of Versailles ended the war in November of that year, President Wilson negotiated a treaty with the European powers that included creating an international League of Nations. Republican Congressman Henry Cabot Lodge was a vigorous opponent of the United States joining the League, because he felt it undercut American autonomy in foreign affairs. Wilson subsequently embarked on a month-long train trip to sell the treaty to citizens across the country. During that train trip, Wilson suffered a stroke that, for all intents and purposes, ended the possibility of American participation in the League, along with Wilson's presidency. Congress did not ratify the treaty, and the United States did not join the League of Nations. By 1920, 48 countries had joined the League, but it was unable to prevent the run-up to World War II and was effectively disbanded when the Second World War broke out.)

While the name "League of Nations" review did not pan out for Mike and Fred Barnes, the actual review certainly did. They first presented the review at Riverview Park on the North Side of Chicago in the summer of 1918. The Barnes brothers' 1918 live show there was the first of its kind at the park. Not only did it demonstrate the viability of the review for large groups of park-goers, it expanded the concept of Riverview Park.

Riverview was originally set up on the banks of the North Branch of the Chicago River near the intersection of what is now Belmont and Western Avenues. In the 1880s, it was originally a skeet shooting club set up by the William Schmidt family, German immigrants who settled on the North Side. It opened to the public on the July Fourth weekend in 1904 as German Sharp-shooter Park, with deer roaming the nearby woods and targets set up on an island in the river. When the park opened, there was nothing for wives and children to do while the men hunted, so in 1906 the owners commissioned a magnificent five-row carousel with 70 horses handcrafted by Swiss and Italian woodcarvers from the Philadelphia Toboggan Coaster company.

Between 1905 and 1920 rides were added to the Park, as well as a ballroom and a roller rink for entertainment during the winter. By the 1920s, Riverview laid claim to being "the world's largest amusement park," exceeding New York's more famous Coney Island.

Riverview Park 1908

Riverview's heyday was in the 1940s through the early 1960s. By the late 1960s, with more families moving to the suburbs and problems with evening violence at the Park, Riverview was foundering. One of the attractions, The African Dip, contributed to the racial animus permeating the Park at the time. The superb reporter/historian for *The Chicago Tribune*, Rick Kogan, described The African Dip, "This 'attraction' featured several high, narrow cages. Black men sat in the cages on wooden slats, shouting insults at spectators. For 25 cents, people could throw three balls at a metal disc attached to the cage. Hit the disc and it collapsed the seat and dumped the black man into chest-high water. Onlookers would howl with delight."

As Kogan recounts, The African Dip closed when the legendary newspaperman Mike Royko wrote a column about it. Kogan included some of Royko's column which makes for ironic reading,

. . . One day, while taking my kids through Riverview, I watched white men tossing balls and causing black men to fall and splash in the water, and my youthful, liberal soul was offended. The next day, I wrote a column about how the African Dip was disgraceful and racist; how it provided whites with malicious joy, while demeaning Negroes, stripping them of dignity; how it had no place in the 1960s, the era of the civil rights movement. And within a few days, the African Dip was no more. The cages were taken down. I had triumphed. The only problem was that about six black men showed up at my office, stood in front of my desk and demanded to know why the hell I had caused them to lose their well-paying jobs. As one of them said: "I was making good money for shoutin' insults at a bunch of honkies and getting a little wet, and most of them couldn't throw good enough to put me in the water one out of every 25 throws." I explained that there were greater moral and social issues involved. And he said something like: "Yeah? Well, what about the moral issue of you getting me fired? What kind of job are you going to get me now?" Unfortunately, I couldn't get them jobs. . . .

Not long after that, Riverview Park closed for good.

But back in 1918, presenting the type of review that the Barnes brothers put together was a completely different form of entertainment for Riverview, and it was a stroke of genius. The review played to large crowds and was a huge success. However, whether that success could be replicated at the venue of state fairs remained to be seen.

57

Mary and Betty Jane

Mike would have his chance to see a little more than a year later, in 1920, at one of the country's largest fairs—The Texas State Fair in Dallas. Meanwhile, despite its ignominious end, for decades Riverview was a special place for millions of people. Many fond memories were created during the Park's 63-year run. And without question, some small degree of credit for the success of Riverview goes to Mike and his brother. Their brilliance and ability to find and promote talent changed the nature of the Park and contributed to its popularity. Were it not for Mike, the memories of those millions of people would not be as rich. The park owners recognized it and displayed their gratitude to Mike. In 2019, 101 years after the Barnes brothers review first appeared on the North Bank of the Chicago River, Mike's daughter, Mary recalled, "My father would take my sister Betty Jane (affectionately known as B.J.) and me to Riverview when we were little and even when we were a little older. When we got there, we would be given two tickets, and B.J. and I could go on any ride at the Park as many times as we wanted. It was such wonderful fun."

Chapter Nine

State Fair

For much of the twentieth century and even before, state fairs were an integral part of the fabric of American life, especially in the Midwest and the South. Whether in the comfortable warmth of May, the oppressive heat of August, or the brisk chill of October, thousands of people would travel from towns large and small to their state capitals and large cities to walk the midway, enjoy the food, see the farm animals, and most especially watch the talented performers who were hired to entertain them. The very name *State Fair* is synonymous with a 1932 bestseller about the Iowa State Fair, a lyrical musical by Rodgers and Hammerstein, as well as several movie versions including the best-known starring Ann-Margret.

The tradition of the state fair dates back to antiquity. Fairs were intervals of peace, when warring tribes agreed to lay down their arms outside the fair locale. During a general truce, they would watch entertainment and trade with each other. The entertainment brought crowds and those crowds attracted merchants, so the fairs became venues for buying and selling, much as they are today.

Even before the mercantile aspects of the fair, they had another purpose in the ancient civilizations of Egypt, Greece, and Ireland. In ancient Egypt, the fair had a religious significance. At fair time, the Egyptians congregated at the burial places of their kings and queens, with the intent of performing rituals. Likewise in ancient Greece, fairs were held concurrently with the funeral games honoring dead kings and warriors. These fairs became the forerunners of the Olympic Games.

The Irish fairs have their own long, illustrious history. One of the most renowned spots in Ireland is the hill of Tailtiu or Tara Hill. The famous Lughnasa (Gaelic) Festival (the Aonach Tailteann) was first held there over 2000 years ago. Tailte was the foster mother of Lugh, an ancient Celtic god and patron of fairs. The Tailte or Teltown Fair was an early harvest festival to honor the spirit of Tailte with the fruits of the first harvest, accompanied by funeral games. Marriages were often arranged at the Teltown Fair. As in Greece, surrounding villages sent their best athletes to compete in a variety of contests, accompanied by poets and story tellers. The Tailteann Games were held until 1169, were revived from 1924 to 1936, and revived again in 1963. The Teltown Fair lasted until 1806.

Other Irish towns and villages held fairs, the most notable of which was the Dublin Fair. It was well known throughout the British Isles for the large crowds and the occasional outbreaks of violence. In 1950, W. W. Baker of *The Kansas City Times* wrote a description by an English traveler who visited a medieval Dublin Fair, "A few fights and broken heads, inseparable from English as well as Irish fairs, of course, always took place, but the crowd was too dense to allow of much damage being done. There was not only no room for 'science' but no room to strike a blow of a real kind from the shoulder and using the toes. We saw no blood flow."

English fairs of the Middle Ages often began with a town crier carrying a huge gilded glove on a pole, shouting throughout the town, "Oyez, oyez, oyez, the fair's begun, the glove is up. No man can be arrested until the glove is taken down." This was a message from the King that peace was to be observed during the time of the fair. The fair became essential to the development of the English theater. In *Love's Labor Lost* William Shakespeare wrote of a comic entertainer, a progenitor of the performer who Mike Barnes would hire for state fairs centuries hence,

> He is wit's peddler, and retails his wares,
> At wakes and wassails, meetings, markets, fairs.

Even before the American Revolution, fairs were held in North America. The tradition was largely forgotten during the late 18th and early 19th centuries, but agricultural gatherings prompted a revival of the state fair. The first established state fairs took place in New York and New Jersey in 1841. Once again during the Civil War, fairs were on hiatus but by the time of Mike Barnes's birth in 1876, there may have been as many as 1500 state, county, and district fairs. The tradition was established.

Mike and Fred took their review, which had been so successful at Riverview in Chicago, to the State Fair of Texas in 1920. The Texas Fair began in Houston in 1870 but was moved to Dallas in 1886. The fair still takes place from the end of September through most of October, later than most state fairs because of the Texas weather. Avoiding the summer heat by delaying the fair is more amenable to large crowds in the early fall. It is

The Return From The Fair. DRAWING BY W. M. CARY PUBLISHED IN HARPER'S
WEEKLY IN 1873

traditionally one of the highlights of the year in Texas and Dallas,
combining several Texas traditions including automobiles (the
fairgrounds has an automobile pavilion and has had an annual
auto show since 1913), fatty and fried foods (including fried pea-
nut butter and jelly sandwiches), and football (the annual rivalry
game between Texas and Oklahoma, the Red River Shootout, has
been played during the fair at the Cotton Bowl). A more infamous tradition, racism, was also part of the Fair for many years,
the low point being a Ku Klux Klan Day in 1923.

The pressure was on Mike and Fred in Dallas in 1920. The
acts would be expensive to transfer to Dallas, and they didn't

know whether their variety show success would translate to fair-grounds in general. Moreover, the State Fair of Texas had been closed in 1918 during World War I, when the Army moved into Fair Park to establish one of their first aviation boot camps, Camp Dick. While the fair resumed in 1919 following the interruption, no one knew if crowds would continue to show up the next year.

The Barnes review turned out to be a huge success in front of large crowds. The opening bill was the "Parade of Nations"—the old Riverview "League of Nations" production—the name change a result of Wilson's failure to convince the United States to join the League. Mike was always something of a history buff, so many of his productions were historically themed. They included "The Last Days of Pompeii" and "The Battle of Chateau Thierry." The Battle of Chateau Thierry was one of the first successful battles the American Expeditionary Force, led by General John "Black Jack" Pershing, fought in World War I. In July 1918, along with French and Belgian forces, the Americans turned back a last gasp German offensive. This turned out to be one of the turning points of the war. Mike's recreation of the battle must have been not only awe-inspiring but one that elicited the patriotism of the crowd. The show finished with a huge fireworks display that Mike organized.

With their triumph at the Texas State Fair, Mike and Fred were on their way. They were poised to become the biggest fair bookers in the country, and this was only the beginning. Through his attention to detail, Mike assumed most of the talent evaluation, show production, and negotiations with fair managements, while Fred was balancing his time between fair booking and financial investing. But while they were coordinating their efforts, they were temporarily sidetracked by a terrible tragedy.

CHAPTER TEN

A Tragedy Intervenes

In 2019, Mike's granddaughter, Betsy Sheridan Collins, recalled when she was a little girl accompanying B.J. Sheridan, her mother and Mike's eldest daughter, to a special plot in Woodlawn Cemetery in Forest Park, west of Chicago. She was only six years old when her grandfather died, and she had only faint memories of him. But her mother took her there, because that was where her grandfather was buried (his grave was later transferred to Palatine next to that of his wife). She saw where her grandfather was buried, but she remembered much more about the cemetery. The plot was guarded by five sculpted granite elephants, their trunks lowered. Betsy remembered walking along the headstones, some of which had names like Baldy and Smiley, others simply labelled Unknown Male or Unknown Female. There is a story behind the plot, known as Showmen's Rest, which The Chicago Tribune *once called "a sort of Valhalla for distinguished members of the outdoor showman's profession."*

AFTER A PROPOSAL FIRST LAUNCHED AT THE 1893 WORLD Columbian Exposition, a group of outdoor showmen meeting at the Saratoga Hotel in Chicago in 1913 founded The Showmen's

The Showmen's League of America logo

League of America. The League is a community of showpeople from all areas of the amusement industry. It is devoted to service and fellowship, and the welfare of all its members. It is the oldest organization of its type in North America, and the Club's first President was Buffalo Bill Cody, the legendary Wild West performer. Both Mike and Fred were initial members of The Showmen's League, and Fred was an early president of the League. Mike is a member of The Showmen's League Hall of Honor.

(Much of the archives of The Showmen's League was destroyed by a fire in 2001, but a remarkable picture still exists. It is the First Annual Ball of The Showmen's League of America, held in 1914 at the Hotel Sherman. A banner hangs on the wall with an image of Buffalo Bill and the caption "Col. Wm. F. Cody, President.")

The League's devotion to its members extended to every facet of those members' lives. Early in the League's history, the

First Showmen's Ball 1914 (note poster of Buffalo Bill in background)

members decided to provide a cemetery for showpeople. For $1500, the League purchased a plot of land at the southern end of Woodlawn and named it Showmen's Rest. The purchase was negotiated in large measure by Fred Barnes. In 1918, the first Chairman of the Cemetery Committee was Lew Nicholas, who owned a monument company, and offered to provide two stone settees, two corner benches and two corner posts at the cemetery lot at no cost to the League.

In a morbid coincidence, in 1918, the same year Showmen's Rest was created, it was called upon following one of the great tragedies in circus history. Fred and Mike had just opened their review at Riverview, but they would be on hand to help at the beginning of Showmen's Rest, after the 1918 train wreck of the Hagenbeck-Wallace Circus.

At the time, the Hagenback-Wallace Circus was the third largest circus in the United States, after Ringling Bros. and Barnum and Bailey (Ringling Bros. actually owned both circuses but ran them separately until 1919.) The Hagenback-Wallace Circus routinely toured around the Midwest and was scheduled to visit Hammond, Indiana, on June 22, 1918. It featured 22 tents and a wide array of acts including lions, tigers, elephants, trapeze artists, and clowns. Hammond was an especially popular stop for the circus, which had visited the town several times, the previous time in 1914. There were advance ads all over the town, and the children of Hammond, recently out of school, waited in eager anticipation. Three circus trains, the first with animals, the second with performers and employees, and a third with a few employees were scheduled to pull into town about 10:00 a.m.

The first train made it into Hammond without incident. Earlier in the morning at about 4:00 a.m. while the second train, carrying about 400 sleeping performers, was heading toward Hammond, it had to make a stop in nearby Ivanhoe to cool an overheated wheel-bearing box. The middle cars of the 26-car train were stopped on a crossover spur between the Gary & Western Railroad tracks and the Michigan City Railroad tracks. Red lights were activated as a warning to any other approaching trains that a train was stopped on the tracks.

With the United States entering World War I early that summer, troops had to be transported from training camps across the country to points of embarkation on the East Coast. The New York Central served to bring soldiers destined for the Allied

Expeditionary Force in France (some of whom may have fought at Chateau Thierry the following month) to the East Coast. When unloaded of their soldiers, the trains would head west again to pick up the next set of troops ordered to go overseas.

It was still pitch black outside and an empty westbound troop train, piloted by engineer Alonzo Sargent, who had previously been fired for sleeping on the job, ran through the red lights on the Gary & Western tracks. A flagman on the circus train noticed that the troop train was not stopping and was in fact picking up steam and heading right for them. He ran down the track waving a flare and finally tried to get the engineer's attention by throwing a flare through the troop train locomotive's window.

The flagman's efforts were to no avail. More than 150 tons of onrushing locomotive plowed into the back of the circus train at full speed. The circus train's passenger cars were made primarily of wood, and the collision ignited a huge fireball accelerated by the circus train's kerosene lamps. The horrific fireball lit up the sky for miles around. Many of those who were not killed by the initial impact were trapped in the wreckage and could not escape the flames. After the wreckage was cleared and everyone was accounted for, the death toll was put at 86.

One of the rescuers, who himself was burned during his rescue attempts, was quoted as saying,

> *I didn't know what to do first. The first woman I came to kept screaming, "Don't touch me! Don't touch me!" The first man said, "Let me be. I'm dying! We saw women burning alive. It was horrible . . . I never want to see a train wreck again."*

Hagenbeck-Wallace Circus Train Wreck 1918

In the investigation and coroner's inquest that followed, the engineer and conductor of the troop train gave different accounts of what happened, so it was impossible to ascertain the exact cause of the crash. The coroner's inquest heard testimony that the engineer ignored the flare thrown at his cab. According to an account by *The Chicago Tribune* of the coroner's inquest that followed, the conductor testified that the engineer told him, "I must have been dozing."

Five days after the accident, 56 of the dead were brought to Woodlawn Cemetery to be buried in Showmen's Rest. Fred and Mike Barnes were among those who made the arrangements to provide a final resting place for the circus performers who died so tragically. Three trucks bore the coffins, and paying respects were

1500 mourners, most of them circus people. Among the floral tributes was one sent by George M. Cohan, the famed song-and-dance man. His parents had toured on the vaudeville circuit. (The story of the Cohan family on the vaudeville circuit is told in the 1942 Jimmy Cagney movie *Yankee Doodle Dandy*.)

The gravestones are arranged in long, narrow rows to commemorate the unbroken line of performers—clowns and tightrope walkers, tumblers and fire-eaters. Five victims, who could be identified, got individual graves. The remains of 48 other victims, so badly burned they couldn't be identified, were buried in a common grave measuring just 25 by 35 feet. "Baldy," "Smiley," "Unknown Male" and "Unknown Female" may have been roustabouts only recently hired, their true names unknown to the survivors.

A week after the funeral, the president of The Showmen's League and successor to Buffalo Bill Cody, John B. Warren, who left a sickbed to attend the burials, himself died. He was buried in Showmen's Rest alongside the victims of the circus fire. Eleven years later, Fred Barnes would be buried there as well.

Amazingly, the Hagenback-Wallace Circus missed only two performances. With so many of its performers gone and others in the hospital, rival circuses lent performers to Hagenback-Wallace to keep its date in Beloit, Wisconsin. Among the audience members were some of the heavily bandaged, burned survivors, who came to give support to their comrades. As a symbol of their devotion to the entertainment community, The Showmen's League of America gathers every Memorial Day at Showmen's Rest to remember their fallen brothers and sisters. The five sculpted elephants there have their trunks lowered. According to circus lore, if an elephant's trunk is up, it's

Showmen's Rest Cemetery

The Hagenbeck-Wallace Circus Train Wreck Monument at Showmen's Rest

Mike and His Daughters Mary and B.J. at Showmen's Rest on Memorial Day c. 1929

a sign of joy or triumph. A lowered trunk is a sign the animal is mourning. As his granddaughter remembered, Mike Barnes was buried at Showmen's Rest until his wife died and his grave was moved next to hers at St. Michael The Archangel Catholic Cemetery in Palatine, Illinois. (Mike still has a headstone at Showmen's Rest.) In his will, Mike Barnes left $1,000 to the cemetery fund of The Showmen's League of America to care for the victims of the Hagenback-Wallace Circus fire and others buried at Showmen's Rest.

Mary Barnes Galvin at Showmen's Rest on Memorial Day 2019

Victims of the Hagenbeck-Wallace Circus Train Wreck

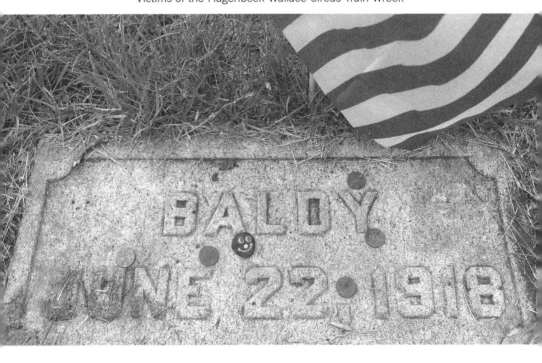

Chapter Eleven

Marriage Between Sweethearts in the Roaring Twenties

The Barnes brothers' triumph at the 1920 State Fair of Texas came at the outset of the Roaring Twenties. Following World War I, the 1920s marked an era of profound societal change. The American economy boomed—between 1920 and 1929, the nation's total wealth more than doubled. For the first time, more Americans lived in cities than on farms. This shift from rural to urban meant that cities now had an important influence on culture and consumerism. Two Constitutional amendments also had a profound effect on culture and consumerism during the Roaring Twenties.

In 1920, the 18th Amendment ushered in Prohibition, formally known as the Volstead Act, which essentially banned the manufacture, sale, and distribution of alcohol. Enforcement of the act proved impossible, and an entire new economy was borne from the public's desire to drink alcohol. In cities, bootlegging, speakeasies, and distilling operations flourished. This new, illegal economy enabled the rapid development of organized crime, especially in New York and Chicago. By the middle of the decade, Johnny Torrio's protégé, Al Capone, was the undisputed king of organized crime in Chicago and arguably the most notorious crime figure in American history. At the height of the Depression in 1933, the public would lose its ardor for Prohibition, and the 18th Amendment would be repealed, the only Constitutional amendment ever to be reversed. Meanwhile, organized crime, entrenched in America, would adjust accordingly, when alcohol was legal again.

Even more important in the long run than the 18th Amendment was the 19th Amendment, ratified in 1920. The 19th Amendment granted American women the right to vote, otherwise known as women's suffrage. The 19th Amendment was the result of decades of protest and lobbying by brave, independent women. In 1848, Elizabeth Cady Stanton and Lucretia Mott organized the Seneca Falls Convention in western central New York. It was the first woman's rights convention, and Ms. Stanton began the convention with a speech on the goals and purposes,

> *We are assembled to protest against a form of government, existing without the consent of the governed—to declare our right to be free as man is free, to be represented in the government which we are taxed to support, to have such disgraceful laws as give man the power to chastise and imprison his wife, to take the wages which she earns, the property which she inherits, and, in case of separation, the children of her love.*

At the convention, women's suffrage became a key part of the women's rights movement. It would take 72 years of difficult struggle, but the efforts of these women, along with others including Susan B. Anthony, finally paid off with the passage of the 19th Amendment, guaranteeing women the right to vote.

During the Roaring Twenties, several new consumer products changed American culture in ways heretofore unimagined. The radio made mass advertising possible and broadened the public's interest in new forms of music and culture, both of which were instrumental in Mike Barnes's plans to provide mass entertainment. The growth of radio in the Twenties was remarkable. In 1920, Pittsburgh's KDKA became the first commercial radio station to broadcast over the airwaves (radio stations east of the Mississippi begin with the call letter W, while those west of the Mississippi begin with the call letter K; KDKA began before the rule was put in place.)

By 1925, there were more than 500 radio stations in America, and by the end of the decade more than twelve million households had radios. People all over the country could listen to the kind of shows Mike was producing and the performers he was promoting. When the fair came to town, after being advertised on radio of course, those people could come and see those acts live.

And they would no longer come to the fair by horse and buggy. Even more remarkable than the spread of the radio was the explosion of the most important consumer product of the decade: the automobile. Thanks in large part to Henry Ford, the Model T, also known as the "Tin Lizzie," changed America. The Model T became the first car that the average citizen could afford, owing to Ford's revolutionary advancements in assembly-line automobile manufacturing. In the 1920s, the Model T (in black–Ford

1920s Ford Model T

famously once said the consumer could have it in any color "as long as it was black" probably because black paint dried fastest on the assembly line and the cars had to be shipped out quickly) was desirable because of its reliability, durability, and affordability. In 1925, the Model T cost about $275, and at that price, more than one-third of all cars sold in the United States were Model T's. For all the people who came to Mike's shows in the 1920s in Model T's, Mike owed at least a small debt of gratitude to Henry Ford.

The automobile provided a newfound freedom, especially to young people. A new generation was driving automobiles and spending money. One of the things they spent money on was music, for listening and dancing. New dances like the Charleston, the Cake Walk, the Lindy Hop (named for Charles Lindbergh) and the Black Bottom swept the nation. Thanks to radio, 100 million phonograph records were sold in 1927 alone.

The 1920s Flapper

After World War I, an African-American migration from the South to Northern urban centers helped spread a new style of music—jazz—across the nation.

The automobile and newfound freedom for women gave them more employment opportunities and financial independence. The "new woman" of the 1920s was known as a "flapper." They wore short skirts, sported bobbed hair, smoked cigarettes, carried hip flasks, listened to jazz, behaved unconventionally, and weren't necessarily disposed to get married. Marriage rates dropped and divorce rates spiked in the 1920s, despite the stigma still attached to divorce.

But Mike went against the decreasing marriage trend of the 1920s. Just a week after returning from Dallas and his triumph at the State Fair of Texas, Mike, who was 44, married Beatrice Mary Meyers, who was 21. The couple was married in Chicago on October 30, 1920. Beatrice was a beautiful, young girl and an accomplished equestrian. While it is not known for sure, it is tempting to speculate that, with their marriage coming so soon after the Texas Fair, Beatrice may have performed in one of Mike's reviews in Dallas.

Although her birth name was Beatrice, Mike always called his wife Billie. This nickname came from her resemblance to Billie Burke, one of the best known and beautiful actresses of the day. Billie Burke made her film debut with the lead role in the 1916 film, *Peggy*. The movie was a hit, and she became a star. Besides her movie work, Billie acted on the Broadway stage, her first love. She was also famous for marrying impresario Flo Ziegfeld of the famous Ziegfeld Follies. Between the two of them, they were quite wealthy, especially with their investments in the booming stock

Beatrice (aka Billie)

market of the 1920s. Billie was able to quit the stage and retire from show business.

Unfortunately, after the stock market crash of 1929, most of the Ziegfeld fortune was wiped out, and Billie had to go back to work. Her most famous role came in 1939 in *The Wizard of Oz*, where she played the Good Witch Glinda. (The story of the marriage of Flo Ziegfeld and Billie Burke is told in a somewhat fictionalized version in the 1936 movie, *The Great Ziegfeld*. Myrna Loy played Billie Burke, William

Billie Burke

Powell played Flo Ziegfeld, and Luise Rainer gave a stunning Academy Award-winning performance as Ziegfeld's first wife.)

Ironically, in the 1920s Mike was becoming the impresario of the state fair, and in fact newspapers referred to him as the "Flo Ziegfeld of the Midwest state fairs." With his own Billie, the two Jazz Age sweethearts would together weather the stock market crash far better than Florenz Ziegfeld and his Billie. Mike and Billie would be married for 36 years until Mike's death, and they had two lovely and successful daughters, B.J. and Mary.

Marriage certificate of Mike and Beatrice (Billie) Oct. 30, 1920

Mike, Billie, and their daughters c. 1925

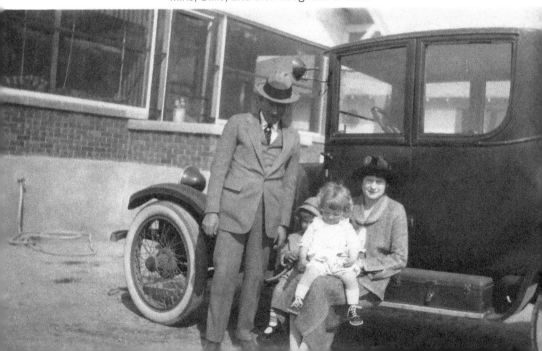

CHAPTER TWELVE

The Bright Lights of Show Business

MARRIAGE AND SUCCESS AT THE TEXAS STATE FAIR PROVIDED Mike a new independence and freed him up to try new ideas. Before he was married, Mike lived with Fred and Fred's daughter Stella on the North Side about a mile from the new Major League baseball park at Clark and Addison where the Chicago Cubs played. That park is known today as iconic Wrigley Field, but when the Barnes family first lived in the neighborhood, the park was known as Weeghman Park. It first opened in 1914 as the home of Charles Weeghman's Federal League team, the Chicago Whales. The Federal League, formed as a rival to the American and National League, quickly folded in 1915.

At that point, the Cubs had been playing in the West Side Grounds on Chicago's near West Side (just outside left field at the West Side Grounds was a psychiatric institution, which gave rise to the expression "out in left field" for someone who is slightly crazy). Weeghman bought the Cubs and moved them to Clark and Addison, and in 1920 he renamed the park Cubs Park. It retained that name until 1926. William Wrigley, the

Weeghman Park c. 1920

chewing gum magnate, bought the Cubs in 1921, and in 1927 he renamed it Wrigley Field.

After they were married, Mike and Billie moved from the Wrigley neighborhood (today known as Wrigleyville) to a more residential neighborhood about a mile farther north at 819 Junior Terrace. Billie soon became pregnant with the couple's first child, B.J. A year later, the couple had their second daughter, Mary. It was a wonderful neighborhood for children, and the girls grew up among the "Junior Terrace Kids," named for the street they lived on.

Mike had big plans for the fair booking business, and he and Fred formed the World Amusement Service Association, with Mike as the president. Mike had attended every convention of the International Association of Fairs and Expositions since he had come to Chicago a decade before, so he certainly

819 Junior Terrace

knew the business, and on many fair decisions Fred deferred to him.

While Fred was primarily an office manager based out of Chicago, Mike threw himself into every aspect of the business. He was unquestionably the best judge of talent in the fair business, and besides auditioning every act—singers, dancers, reviews, circus performers, Wild West acts—he was always on the lookout for new talent. He did not confine himself to the United States; he was beginning to produce shows in Canada so he looked for Canadian performers, and he would frequently travel to Europe for the best European acts that might translate well to Midwestern audiences. If he was not directing a show in rehearsal at the site where it was due to perform, he was busy booking ahead.

The Junior Terrace Kids

But that was only the half of it. He knew every line and every cue. He would walk the fairgrounds, examining every dressing room and every stage, checking with every stagehand. If there was a problem anywhere on the fairgrounds, he knew about it. And he left his mark: toothpicks. Even though he was in control of everything, nerves caused him to chew toothpicks and leave them everywhere—in the dressing rooms, around the stage, under the grandstand, and on the race track. If there were broken toothpicks on the grounds, it was a sure bet Mike Barnes was somewhere close by. In the early days, he started chewing wooden matchsticks, but because he didn't smoke, it became embarrassing to ask his friends who did smoke for matches. Because every restaurant carried toothpicks, he switched over and continued to chew them the rest of his life. As one newspaper put it, "he blazed toothpick trails."

The highlights of many of his early 1920s shows were the silent, poorly illuminated production numbers like "The Last Days of Pompeii" with fireworks displays at the end of the evening. But Mike realized that fireworks and silent productions would not sustain a show. So he made a quantum leap in producing fairs—with sound and light.

Before this, the fairs essentially closed down after sundown. There was poor lighting and sound amplification basically came from megaphones. Then Mike met Ralph Hemphill, and the two became friends and worked together revolutionizing the fair concept. Ralph Hemphill was the manager of the Oklahoma State Fair, and together Mike and Ralph introduced the loudspeaker, which along with new stage lighting made huge nighttime grandstand shows possible. The nighttime grandstand show, no longer silent, replaced the fireworks show as the highlight of the evening.

Mike Barnes Blazing Toothpick Trails

Years later, Mike would reminisce to *The Kansas City Star* about the revolutionary aspects of introducing improved sound and lighting, "I really think we hit our stride in 1925 when we got sound amplifying equipment that would really work. From there, the show kept on growing with improvements and lighting equipment and in staging effects." He went on to tell *The Star* that the big improvements in lighting, made in experiments at fair grandstands, helped the outdoor show business to spread into regular outdoor theaters like The Starlight Theater in Kansas City.

With these advances, the work of Mike and Ralph Hemphill may have been more influential than even they could have anticipated. Now that there was activity at night, crowds swelled to the tens of thousands at many state fairs. This, in turn, necessitated even larger sound systems and lighting setups. In many respects, this paved the way for the large outdoor rock concerts of a generation later. The Who, The Rolling Stones, The Eagles and all the other legendary rock acts that played large venues and stadiums owe a debt of gratitude to Mike Barnes and Ralph Hemphill. In fact, the greatest rock act of them all actually played a Midwestern state fair.

Of all the thousands of acts that have played in all the fairs over the last two centuries, there is no question that one act stands above all the rest.

On September 3, 1964, on their second North American tour, The Beatles played two shows on the Indianapolis State Fairgrounds at the Indiana State Fair. The Beatles broke on the American scene in spectacular fashion in February 1964, with three television appearances on CBS's *The Ed Sullivan Show*. At that time, they only made live appearances in New York

City, Washington D.C., and Miami. But in the late summer of 1964, as a result of their popularity and promotion for their first movie, *A Hard Day's Night*, they did a more extensive tour of the United States including several Midwestern cities, as well as Toronto and Montreal.

The Indiana State Fair was the only state fair they played (although they did play in Dallas at the Texas State Fairgrounds on that same tour, but that was before the opening of the fair that year). The advances Mike Barnes made in state fair production made it possible for rock and roll acts to tour state fairs in the late 1950s and 1960s. Elvis Presley played at the Texas State Fair in 1956, and package tours of performers were regularly organized to travel to state fairs across the country. The Caravan of Stars, assembled by Dick Clark of *American Bandstand* fame, was probably the most well-known of these package tours. (The 1996 Tom Hanks movie, *That Thing You Do!*, is a fairly accurate, albeit fictional, portrayal of the rock act package tour that played state fairs.)

But no package tour of rock performers at any state fair ever had any act like The Beatles. (There were other acts on the bill that day including Jackie DeShannon and Clarence "Frogman" Henry.) The Beatles performed a standard 12-song set twice, once in the early evening and the second time at night. All told, both shows together drew over 29,000 people, primarily teenagers. The two concerts netted The Beatles $85, 231.93 with $1,719.02 deducted for state income tax. They stayed at The Speedway Motel and their contract rider read, "we would appreciate it very much if the dressing room could be equipped with a supply of clean towels, chairs, a case of Coca-Cola, and if at all possible a portable TV set."

The Beatles at the Indiana State Fair 1964

(Ironically, The Beatles would stop playing live shows two years later, because the stadium sound systems of the day, pioneered in part forty years previously by Mike Barnes, could no longer accommodate their performances.)

In 1964, The Beatles, while extremely popular, were not yet the international phenomenon they would become shortly afterward. It would have been interesting to know what the biggest rock stars in the world thought, much later in life, of playing at a Midwestern State Fair. The only indication we have of their impressions was by George Harrison, an avid car enthusiast. In his 1992 book, *Anthology*, he wrote,

> *Indianapolis was good. As we were leaving, on the way to the airport, they took us round the Indy circuit, the 500 Oval, in a Cadillac. It was fantastic. I couldn't believe how long the straightway was; and to be on the banking and see all the grandstands was great.*

Just as interesting as The Beatles' reaction to playing the Indiana State Fair would have been Mike's reaction to them playing there. He died about a year before John Lennon was introduced to Paul McCartney at a Liverpool church, but as the consummate showman, Mike probably would have been happy to see the biggest act in the world at a state fair—and quite proud.

CHAPTER THIRTEEN

The Hippodrome Experience

IN 1928, MIKE AND FRED DISSOLVED THE WORLD AMUSEMENT Service Association. Mike was looking to put on bigger shows at more fairs, while Fred was shifting his attention away from fair booking and more toward investing. The brothers teamed with a man named Ed Carruthers and started the legendary Barnes-Carruthers Theatrical Enterprises. Sam J. Levy Sr. and Fred H. Kressman functioned as senior staffers in the Chicago office. With better lighting and sound now available for fairgrounds, Mike argued for more revue-type shows, an idea that met with some resistance among members of the new organization, including Fred.

What Mike was proposing was a huge financial gamble. Large revue shows were expensive to produce and travel. No doubt Mike's partners were deterred by the disastrous experience of the Hippodrome Theater in New York—and with some reason.

The Hippodrome Theater, also known as the New York Hippodrome, opened in 1905. Located on Sixth Avenue between 43rd and 44th Streets in the Midtown Manhattan Theater District, it was billed as the largest theater in the world, seating

5,200, with a stage twelve times larger than any Broadway counterpart. When it opened it was known as "The Jewel of New York." (The hippodrome was an ancient Greek stadium used for horse racing and chariot racing. The term comes from the Greek words for horse "hippos" and course "dromos." The Roman equivalent was called a "circus" and the most well-known was the "Circus Maximus." The largest hippodrome in the Ancient World was in Constantinople and seated more than 60,000.)

Built by the creators of Luna Park, the famed amusement park at Coney Island, The Hippodrome could hold an entire circus, complete with horses, elephants, and 1,000 performers. The stage also had huge glass water tanks that could be raised and lowered for water and diving shows. From its opening in 1905 through World War I, The Hippodrome featured huge, lavish shows and stage productions. There were elaborate spectacles, hundreds of chorus girls, and horses diving into the large water tanks. Perhaps the most famous act to ever perform at The Hippodrome occurred in 1918, when the legendary illusionist Harry Houdini performed his "Vanishing Elephant" trick, making Jenny, a full-grown elephant, disappear on stage before thousands of people. The trained elephant entered a huge cabinet onstage and seemingly vanished in front of the audience. (Houdini played at The Hippodrome for nineteen weeks, his longest run at any single theater in his career.)

For fifteen years, The Hippodrome was a huge success. But by the early 1920s (exactly when Mike was gearing up shows for Midwestern fairs), financial considerations overwhelmed The Hippodrome. Even with its huge seating capacity, the theater could not draw enough customers to support its tremendous operating costs. A succession of producers and owners failed to keep the theater profitable, and in 1923 the owners turned to featuring

Houdini and Jenny the Elephant at the Hippodrome

vaudeville acts. Such a large theater was not conducive to vaude-ville, and in any event, vaudeville was slowly being shunted aside by the motion pictures. The Hippodrome then attempted to com-bine vaudeville acts with showing movies, but the competition was too stiff from movie houses all over New York City that were specially designed for that purpose and operated more profitably.

In 1928, less than a decade from its days as the world's great-est theater, The Hippodrome went dark. In 1935, producer Billy

Rose leased the empty theater for his Rodgers and Hart circus musical, *Jumbo*. Despite favorable reviews, the musical lasted less than six months, a victim of the dire economic conditions of the Depression. This was the death knell for The Hippodrome—the final curtain as it were. The building was demolished in 1939.

The rapid decline of The Hippodrome, especially during the 1920s, must have sent a frisson of fear through producers across the country. Most of them probably believed that there was no longer a place for large spectacles featuring elaborate shows, circus animals, hundreds of performers, singers, and dancers. The Hippodrome experience demonstrated the costs and competition from the movies would not permit it.

This is where Mike Barnes was such a visionary. He understood, and was able to convince his Barnes-Carruthers partners, that what happened at the Hippodrome proved no such thing. While state fairs could not charge the high admission fees that were common to New York and there were travel costs to factor in, many things would work in favor of having those shows at state fairs. Rents and lodging costs for acts and animals were much lower than in Manhattan. The fairgrounds did not need heating and maintenance, and costs would be negligible in the offseason, unlike at The Hippodrome. In addition, the potential audiences were much larger. A couple of thousand tourists and New Yorkers might come once for an evening at The Hippodrome, but tens of thousands of fairgoers anxious to see shows would come for several weeks to the state fair. Mike Barnes knew that, The Hippodrome notwithstanding, he could make the elaborate production work at the state fair. It would take lots of work by Mike, but before that, there would be unforeseen problems.

CHAPTER FOURTEEN

1929

As it was for so many people, 1929 was a bad year for Mike. Most importantly, on June 2 his brother Fred died at the age of 58. (Fred is buried at Showmen's Rest right next to The Showmen's League President John Warren, who died right after the circus train wreck.) This was a blow to Mike, because while he and Fred had not always agreed on business strategy, it was Fred who convinced him to come to Chicago and who had gotten him started in the fair booking business. Mike had acted as the secretary for Fred's company, F.M. Barnes Inc. (In 1920, Mike purchased four three-story brownstones in a North Side German neighborhood for $50,000 for F.M. Barnes Inc. He promptly turned them into a three-story apartment hotel worth $750,000.)

Before he got married, Mike had even lived with Fred and his daughter Stella near North Lake Shore Drive. Daughter Stella became the head of the contract department of the Music Corporation of America (MCA) in New York. She died in 1949 at the age of 46. Because MCA was founded as a music booking agency in Chicago in 1924, it is likely that Fred was responsible for Stella's connection to MCA. Fred, five years Mike's senior,

Fred Barnes with his nieces, B.J. and Mary

was also listed in a 1917 edition of *The Billboard*, in an alphabetical list of Members of National Vaudeville Artists, Inc., so he may have started his career as a vaudeville performer.

Besides being a managing partner of Barnes-Carruthers Theatrical Enterprises, Fred Barnes was the seventh president of The Showmen's League of America from 1925–1926. Fred had been one of The Showmen League leaders in the purchase of Showmen's Rest, which proved so important after the Hagenbach-Wallace Circus Fire. After the fire, Fred was instrumental in Showmen League programs that still exist to help showpeople who have undergone misfortune. Today, those activities include providing scholarships for students, financial aid, and memorial services. There is also a special park in Florida set up for show people in the winter.

Nineteen twenty-nine also presented the greatest challenge of Mike Barnes's business career, only a year after Barnes-Carruthers Theatrical Enterprises was formed. It was the year The Roaring Twenties and the economic boom ended and the Great Depression began. It started with the stock market crash in October, with the average value of 50 leading stocks falling by almost half in two months.

Although the advent of the Depression was probably obvious in retrospect, no one saw it coming at the time. Poor regulatory policies meant many banks were overextended. Agriculture had collapsed after World War I, and the collapse had gone unnoticed during the Twenties boom but remained a source of economic weakness. Although profits were good for most of the decade, wages failed to keep pace and the ability of consumers to borrow and spend had reached its limits. There were signs of trouble late in the decade when production began to decline and unemployment started to rise. Finally, stock prices had far exceeded the real value of companies.

Once the market began to decline, both investors and consumers lost confidence at ever-growing rates. Every negative trend began feeding on itself, and the government led by newly elected President Herbert Hoover, was powerless to do anything. If anything, Hoover's policies, which included stiff tariffs on imported goods, aggravated the situation. By 1933, the stock market had fallen by 75 percent compared to its 1929 highs, and unemployment hovered at 25 percent. It was hardly an auspicious time for any business, let alone one that depended on the average fairgoer's discretionary income. The Great Depression drastically increased the gamble Mike was taking by selling expensive fair shows. The Hippodrome, after all, failed during the flush times of the mid-1920s. With the worst economic conditions the country had ever faced, no end in sight, and now with Fred gone (and Ed Carruthers would die six years later in 1935, also buried at Showmen's Rest), could Mike's business plans succeed?

Fortunately, Mike had been in a similar situation before, having survived the Panic of 1907. While this was an even worse economic catastrophe, Mike knew to keep a level head, even as he grieved his brother's death. He would not waver on his early business principle that if you are familiar with a business, back your judgment to the maximum and commit all the brains and money you have available to make it succeed.

CHAPTER FIFTEEN

Beating the Odds Once More in Oklahoma and Kansas

DURING THE DEPRESSION, WHERE OTHERS FAILED, MIKE Barnes succeeded. He did so through a combination of financial acumen, good judgment, the ability to negotiate and form relationships. The skills he learned everywhere from the Lower East Side of Manhattan to the Chicago Loop paid off handsomely in the 1930s. One of the keys to his success was shrewd appraisal of how likely the fairs he worked with would do well. He said, "You know how to spot an act with public appeal and you're in business." But he was cautious and made sure not to provide shows to fairs that could not carry them financially. As he pointed out, "That's why our losses from fairs that couldn't pay off have been infinitesimal."

The Depression began in the late fall of 1929, so 1930 was the first fair season that would test Barnes-Carruthers Theatrical Enterprises. Once again, Mike took a calculated gamble. His key fair of the 1930 season would be the Oklahoma State Fair, where he worked with his friend, Ralph Hemphill. Over the years, Mike had cultivated relationships and made friends with many people in Oklahoma City including bankers, stock and commodity brokers, and hotel operators. These people trusted him, and their help and financial support for the Fair helped minimize his risk. Mike had been using light systems and speakers since 1925 in Kansas, but Ralph Hemphill had been looking for the right opportunity to use a more sophisticated loud speaker system and advanced lighting to put on huge, nighttime grandstand shows and transform the Oklahoma State Fair. He and Mike decided together that the 1930 Oklahoma Fair was their chance. They put on a show called "The Awakening" and it was a tremendous success.

People in Oklahoma may not have had much money in 1930, but what they had, they were willing to spend at the state fair. And Mike's nighttime grandstand shows, which were free, became a prime attraction. That 1930 show became the template for nighttime grandstand shows in other states. And as Mike once said, "I've never lost a show once the customers got into the grandstand. We'll put on something as long as they want to stay."

Another fair that cemented Mike Barnes's reputation during the Depression was the Kansas Free Fair, held in Topeka. It was the first free fair in the country, but in 1931 it went bankrupt. The Fair was rescued by a bombastic, table-pounding businessman named Maurice Jencks. Over the next 20 years, Michael Barnes and Maurice Jencks would develop a love/hate relationship, as Mike helped Maurice restore the Kansas Free Fair to its place as one of the best in the country.

When Jencks took over the Kansas Free Fair as manager in 1932, it owed $92,000. Over the next two decades, he paid off the debt, put more than a million dollars in permanent buildings and improvements, and turned a profit. All

Maurice Jencks of the Topeka Free Fair

this was done without changing the fair structure by charging a fee at the gate—admission was still free. Under his operation, the fair never failed to make money, despite the Depression, droughts, tornadoes, and other potential setbacks. When asked how he did it, he said, "Don't give them anything but good entertainment." And that meant Mike Barnes.

Mike made it a point to make the week of the Topeka Fair his top priority. He would come several days early, arriving before the baggage cars loaded with lighting equipment, scenery, and costumes. He was responsible for 175 persons connected with the show. Because of the frequency of summer thunderstorms and tornadoes (remember, Kansas is *Wizard of Oz* territory), Mike had to employ scenery that could be easily put up and taken down but would stand up to the torrential rains. "We generally play to between 70,000 and 100,000 people during the nights we play in Topeka."

Mike lost $25,000 the first few years he did the Topeka Fair, but he never considered abandoning it, even when he had better offers during the week of the fair. He would joust throughout the year with Maurice Jencks, but they would always make a deal by fair time because of their mutual respect. Of Jencks, Mike said, "Now don't tell him I told you, but there isn't a fair manager in America who can touch Maurice Jencks. His judgment is recognized throughout the fair world. There are dozens of fairs over the United States today patterned after his Topeka show. Now this week I have several shows running. But never would I miss Topeka—never. In most cities, I manage my shows from my hotel room—not in Topeka. Here, I even sell tickets when the crowds are hammering at the gates. I'm on the lot from morning until night. It is a privilege to work with a man like Maurice Jencks."

Mike Barnes of the Topeka Free Fair

Jencks felt the same about Mike, "The greatest showman on any lot anywhere today is Mike Barnes. His shows are the tops in every big fair in the country today—sometimes he is operating three or four at a time." The fights between the two men were legendary, but during the depths of the Depression, two closer allies could not be found. They survived when many others could not. As *The Kansas City Star* put it,

> *To hear the pair arguing over acts and tents and stage construction and tickets and labor expense, a casual observer would expect gunfire at any moment. But if one ever detected the other was in need of help, he would leap at the chance to be of service. A great pair—Michael Barnes and Maurice Jencks.*

TOPEKA--We Thank You!

Two paramount features go to make a successful state fair— education and entertainment.

For nearly a quarter of a century it has been our pleasure and privilege to attempt to match the educational advantages of the Kansas Free Fair with entertainment.

Our only yardstick of success is the measurement of public patronage.

The shattering of records this heated and dry week has proved to us your appreciation of our efforts. The fact that you have packed the grandstand, night after night, day after day, indicates that we have served you successfully.

We leave Topeka after the night show this evening with gratitude in our hearts for your sincere approval of our part of this great institution, known all over the United States and Canada, the "Free Fair of Kansas."

Your enthusiasm, displayed at our shows, has inspired all of us—to the last employe, to the final actor, and actress, we have met your applause with renewed efforts to please.

We leave for our next engagement with deeply imbedded memories of our stay on the Kansas Free Fair grounds.

We cannot leave without expressing, in this manner, our sincere appreciation of your reception, your spirit, your grand fair and all its displays and exhibits, your city and your management, led by that great master of all showmen, recognized thruout America, Maurice W. Jencks.

It is our only hope that we may be with you again next year.

"Mike" Barnes

BARNES-CARRUTHERS FAIR BOOKING ASSOCIATION
Chicago, Ill.

Mike's "thank you" to Topeka

CHAPTER SIXTEEN

A View of Barnes-Carruthers
from the Federal Writers Project

In 1932, in the wake of the Depression, Franklin Delano Roosevelt was elected president, replacing Herbert Hoover. Almost immediately upon taking office, Roosevelt instituted the New Deal, a series of projects and programs to repair the economy and provide jobs to the unemployed. As part of the New Deal, The Works Progress Administration, known as the WPA, instituted the WPA Federal Writers Project. This program was designed to provide jobs for unemployed writers, editors, and researchers. At its height, the project employed 6,000 men and women. At one time or another, then-unknown but later to be famous writers who took part in the project included Saul Bellow, Studs Terkel, Nelson Algren, and Ralph Ellison. The writers delved into and wrote travelogues and guides to every state and other subjects, including local histories, nature studies, and folklore connections.

One of the authors, Alfred O. Phillipp, wrote several pieces for the Folklore Section called Chicago Folkstuff about vaudeville

WPA Federal Writers Project

in Chicago. He also wrote a manuscript entitled Fair Booking Agency, an interview he did with a local performer-turned manager (who coincidentally happened to be a Cook County Democratic Precinct Committeeman). The interview describes the fair booking business, an encounter at the Barnes-Carruthers Fair Booking Association during the Depression, and a mention of Mike Barnes. It gives useful historical context to the business Mike was in during the Depression.

The manuscript was published in 1940 as part of the WPA Federal Writers Project and is housed today in the Library of Congress in Washington D.C. This is an edited, abbreviated version of that interview.

The particular clinic in which we will conduct our research is the BARNES-CARRUTHERS FAIR BOOKING ASSO-CIATION—occupying the entire fifth floor of the Grand Opera House Building, at 121 North Clark St. This veteran firm is the sole survivor of a long list of fair booking agencies that flourished in Chicago during the "good old days," before Major Bowes and the vaudeville agents horned in.

Let's turn to the acts themselves, the performers, the actual workers and producers who are across the street from the County Building, at 121 North Clark Street. Into an old elevator, and up to the fifth floor, where we emerge into the spacious offices of the Barnes-Carruthers Fair Booking Association. There is a small waiting room separated from the large main office by a low railing, and the sole furnishing of this waiting room consists of a hard bench with a seat highly polished through continual contact with the pants of the job seeking acrobats and aerialists. There are two or three chairs, less highly polished, but equally hard. The low railing affords an unobstructed view of the entire main office. Near the gate sits the usual pretty girl at an information desk and switchboard. Out of sight, in smaller offices, sit E. F. Carruthers and M. H. Barnes, the heads of the firm (note: E. F. Carruthers had died by the time described).

Sam. J. Levy, general secretary and all-around handy man, presumably has a desk somewhere; but his continual activity in every part of the office precludes the possibility of locating it. A meagre complement of clerks and stenographers completes the office personnel.

Time—the spring of 1939, which Chicago is celebrating (on April 10th.) with a snowstorm. We pour ourselves out of the elevator and into the small waiting room. The room was far more crowded than is usual at this time of year. Many were performers that I knew, pals of former years; but there were a few new faces, acts that were strangers to me.

"Hello Alfredo, what are you doing here?" Paul Armento greeted me. "You've a stranger around the booking offices, aren't you?"

"Yeah, I just dropped in to say hello." I answered evasively. "You're looking good. How are you tumbling these days, still got your old speed?" "Well, I'm not exactly burning up the pad, but I can still turn over," Paul was a mighty tumbler in his day. "I'm pulling more of the easy routines now, like boranis and tinsikis (trampoline maneuvers); but I'm still doing backs in a swing, and I can still pick up a high full."

"Who're you working with?"

"I'm doing a three-act with a couple of kinkers (circus performers). Don Ray and Joe Samuels, maybe you know 'em. Comedy acrobatic with a table rock finish."

"Say, Paul, isn't that Nick Machedon over in the corner? Used to do triple bars with his brother,—the Machedon Brothers."

"Yeah, that's Nick. He's still doing a stick act."

"Last time I worked with Nick was on the Bell Circuit," I reflected. "We toured Mexico together in 1927–28. I remember his knockout finish; somersault over the middle bar, kip- up, into giant swings, and a double away,—all in swing time. It was sure a flash routine. Can he still clear the middle bar?" "Oh, he still manages to get from end-bar to end-bar," Paul answered. "But he's cut the somersault; just does a fly-over now. And, of course, he's slowed down. You know, Alfredo, there's so little work now that an act can't keep in trim anymore."

Also in the crowded room were–"Perrone & Ricardo, Sensational High Perch Act,"—Paul Lorenzo, owner and manager of "The Four Lorenzos,"—"Aerial Larkins," a man and woman double trap act,—Earl Wright, owner and manager of "Wright's Canines,"—Hoshi Taketa, manager of a troupe of Japanese acrobats,—Gus Gerbin, of "The Six Demascos, Arabian Whirlwind Tumblers,"—"Hi Hubert, Sensational Cloud Swing,"—an assortment of clowns and several artists unknown to me.

Fair booking agencies do not secure employment (or engagements) for individual artists, except in such cases where the lone artist does a "single," i.e., an act by himself.

The fair agency is in the business of placing only complete acts which are ready (produced and rehearsed) to perform before the public. In the case of acrobatic troupes, or other large acts, it is only the owner or manager of the act who makes the continuous rounds of the agents' offices. Acts wherein all members work on the commonwealth plan (splitting salaries equally) one of the partners is usually chosen to "do the business for the act."

"Say, what are all these joeys (clowns) doing here?" I asked Hubert.

"Trying to horn in on the Stadium show," Hubert replied. "You mean that Cirque Olympe, or so-called Greater European Circus, that's going to open at the Chicago Stadium next week. Who's putting it on?"

"The Stadium Corporation itself is running the show, but I guess they're using mostly all Barnes-Carruthers acts."

"Don't worry, old Mike Barnes has got a finger in the promotion," asserted Nick Machedon.

"Barnes has to hustle and promote dates to keep his acts in chow money so they'll still be alive by the time the fair season opens," commented Hubert. "Remember how we used to book fairs in the old vaudeville days? I remember I always used to sign up with Mike Barnes for the following year, I'd bring my photos, cuts, and catalogue matter up here and then forget about it. I'd go out and play vaudeville, and this office would never see me again until it was time to open on the fairs."

"Say, do you think vaudeville will ever come back?" a young chap inquired innocently.

Vaudeville was not coming back, but this WPA piece, while perhaps overly long, provides an idea of the type of acts that Mike Barnes would interview and audition all year long everywhere from the Chicago Loop to Canada to Europe. There was every manner of circus act, elephants, opera stars, Wild West shows, drama revues, chorus lines, and women and men shot out of cannons. But in his long career, Mike did have some favorites.

CHAPTER SEVENTEEN

Some of Mike's Most Notable Acts

THE KANSAS STATE FAIR, ONE OF MIKE'S FAVORITE AND MOST popular shows, showcased the variety of Mike's grandstand acts. The Kansas State Fair took place annually in Hutchinson, Kansas. This was a separate fair from the Free Fair in Topeka.

(One of the frequent visitors to the Fair was Kansas Governor Alf Landon. He is best known for running for president against Franklin D. Roosevelt, and losing in one of the most one-sided elections in history, winning only eight electoral votes, those of Maine and Kansas. A popular magazine of the day, *Literary Digest*, predicted in a poll that Landon would win, but their poll was based on a selected sample from telephone directories of likely Republican voters. *Literary Digest* folded shortly after its disastrous prediction.)

The highlight of the Kansas Fair was Mike's *opus magnum*, "The World On Parade." As *The Kansas City Star* described it, "'The World On Parade' is truly superb entertainment, and is hereby recommended to every man, woman and child in the Sunflower State . . . between 8,000 and 9,000 saw 'The World On Parade' open to the roar of a tri-motored airplane which carries the audience to Deauville, France, then to Nice, then to Moscow. From Russia to the most oriental section of India. Then one goes to Spain and the land of the gay senorita and back to Colonial Days of the Thirteen Colonies. The finale is as stirring a Washington bi-centennial tribute as Kansas will see." (Mike's shows invariably contained a patriotic tribute to the United States.)

Besides "The World On Parade," the grandstand show included the Metropolitan operatic quartet, including performers from the Chicago Civic Opera. There was a musical comedy act, the Foster Dancers, who also performed on Broadway. The act included 30 chorus girls with dazzling costumes from "the far corners of the world." The revue included an "ice show" on a chemically prepared floor that gave the appearance of ice. This was followed by a troupe of Arabian tumbling artists, acrobatic dancers, animal acts, pole sitters and bands.

And Mike supervised each act meticulously. The reviews were glowing. As *The Kansas City Star* reporter covering the fair wrote, "Once in a great while there comes an entertainment where the plaudits of the severest critic are more flowery than the encomiums of the advance publicity man and deservedly so."

Mike could reasonably lay claim to having contracted more novelty acts and thrill attractions than anyone else in America. But of all his acts, he always maintained his biggest fair attraction was Captain F. F. Frakes. The Captain would fly out of the sky in a fast airplane and crash through a house specially erected in front of the grandstand. He would fly the plane fast enough that both the house and plane would be destroyed, but he would invariably walk away unharmed.

Captain Frank "Bowser" Frakes, also known as "Fearless Frakes," was a Tennessee stunt pilot who came up with the idea

F. F. Frakes Crashes A Jenny Into a Building

of staging airplane crashes. The show's origins most likely began before the turn of the century when an Ohio railroad company devised a publicity stunt: a collision between two obsolete trains filled with dummy passengers and ticket collectors. On a rainy afternoon in 1896, 25,000 people came to watch the trains collide at full speed on the tracks.

Twenty-five years later, the owner of an Ohio aerobatic flight school put on a show of daredevil automobile drivers who displayed their driving skills. The highlight of the performance turned out to be the wrecks and smashes—autos colliding in head-on crashes, slamming into brick and flaming walls, leaping from ramps straight into other vehicles (the "T-bone Crash"), and running over human "iron men." This was the forerunner of the demolition derby, still popular today.

Throughout the 1920s and 1930s, barnstorming pilots like Capt. Frakes employed the same entertainment concept with airplanes. Barnstorming became especially popular in the 1920s when the American government found itself with a surplus of old World War I aircraft. Without any use for these planes, the government sold them to civilians, who were usually former aviators or old-time pilots.

Based on the popularity of the automobile daredevils, pilots with light planes could entertain the public at a low cost (at least from a financial standpoint it was low, the physical risk would often be significant, and not surprisingly stunt pilots had a high mortality, one of the problems that forced the government to intervene). Early on, the pilots would travel through small towns, taking people who had never been on planes for rides. Soon, the pilots moved on to performing dangerous stunts as a whole village watched. Word spread quickly from town to town, and barnstorming pilots became local heroes. Some even became national heroes.

Mike employed Capt. Frakes for state fairs because the pilot was among the top daredevils of the day. Frakes sought out old planes that he could buy cheaply, usually World War I Curtiss Jennys, JN biplanes made by the Curtiss Aeroplane Company, developed as training aircraft for the Army. With some repair work he rendered them airworthy—for one flight only into some trees or a lake. As one observer described it, "Bowser came into sight over the treetops, with his wings wagging, and slewing from side to side as if something was badly wrong with the airplane. He would cut the power, then pull on the choke to make the small engine cough and belch out puffs of smoke. Within seconds, every eye in the stands was fixed on the struggling airplane. The crowd held its breath, and a few women screamed." But he always emerged unscathed.

Frakes decided to make his act even more dramatic by flying his planes into prefabricated houses, specially constructed with two-by-fours and siding, and measuring about 16 by 30 feet. Mike caught a performance, loved the act, and predicted that fair audiences would love it as well.

Frakes explained the secret of his act to *The Reading Eagle*, "I admit I fool the public," he said. "Everybody who goes out there will expect to see me get killed, but I won't. Just the same, they won't be disappointed. I'll show them the most spectacular stunt they ever witnessed. The secret is that I never let that engine crankshaft hit anything solid. I don't care what happens to the rest of the plane. Let 'er rip."

As usual, Mike was spot on in his prediction that Captain Frakes would be a hit. "Fearless Frakes" became a national celebrity; at one point he was even a pitchman for Camel cigarettes. His presence on fair programs increased attendance by thousands—another Barnes masterstroke. At the 1937 Iowa State Fair, he drew 62,500: 24,500 in the filled grandstand and another 38,000 standing outside the track fence. One year at the Ohio State Fair, he drew 60,000 to a show that also featured "Lucky Lindy," Charles Lindbergh. The only sticking point was the Civil Aeronautics Authority (CAA), which frowned on Captain Frakes's stunts. The CAA was always trying to revoke his pilot's license. Somehow, he managed to avoid them at every turn. A good illustration was a small U.P. story that once ran across the wires during the Nebraska State Fair for which Mike had hired him,

A plane crash before a Nebraska State Fair crowd yesterday proved expensive for Capt. F. F. Frakes, stunt flyer or his agent when Frakes pleaded guilty to an air traffic violation and was fined $150 and costs by City Judge John A. McGuire. Frakes admitted flying at an altitude of less than 500 feet over a congested area contrary to law.

When World War II broke out, Frakes joined the Royal Canadian Air Force. Too old for combat, he flew cargo planes, and when the United States entered the war, he returned home as a flight instructor for the U.S. Army Air Forces. Despite all the crashes he was involved in over his career, Fearless Frakes died in 1970 of old age.

Mike also explained that while Captain Frakes was his single biggest attraction, his second biggest attraction was Lillian Boyer, also known as "The Girl of Nerve," "The Aerial Sensationalist," and "The Empress of the Air." Throughout the 1920s, the petite Lillian performed at Mike's fairs in a Curtis Jenny biplane flying above the crowd and hanging by one hand, by her knees or ankles, wing walking, or standing on the top wing while the pilot looped the loop.

Her repertoire also included transferring from a speeding automobile to an airplane (she was the first woman to do so); transferring from plane to plane; hanging by one hand from the skid under a wing tip; balancing on her head; standing, her feet under a strap, while the pilot looped the old flying machine once or twice; doing stunts on a ladder, and parachute drops. (Many

Lillian Boyer Performing "The Breakaway"

of the stunts Lillian performed are portrayed in the 1975 Robert Redford film about barnstormers, *The Great Waldo Pepper*.)

But her greatest and most dangerous stunt was what she called "The Breakaway"—hanging from the flying plane by her teeth. Near the end of her life, she described the stunt to *The Los Angeles Times*, "It was the surprise. When I'd leave the cockpit I would take a strong, thin cable with me and attach it to a strut." Her mouthpiece was on it, and the pilot could reel in the cable from his cockpit. But the spectators, watching from 3,000 feet below, did not know that. "After I'd do a few things on the tip of the lower wing, I'd put the mouthpiece in and climb over the wing to the skid, do one thing and another and then hang there a minute and let go. The 'Ahs' and 'Ohs' would start. They thought I was falling. Then, the cable would go taut and I'd hang here under the plane, do a spread eagle and other tricks. As long as my weight was on the cable, there was no way I could open my mouth. Then, Mr. Brock (the pilot) would lower the ladder and I'd grab it, let go of the mouthpiece, and do a few more tricks on the way up." Although she would have died immediately if the cable broke, "I was never afraid. I don't know if I lacked good sense or what. But I never had any fear at all. I never left the ground without a prayer to God, though, and, when I returned, I thanked Him."

Mike could only employ Lillian through the 1920s. After the 352 wing walking shows, 143 airplane to automobile transfers, and 37 parachute jumps, Lillian was forced to retire by the Government. Federal regulations against barnstorming acts like hers ended her daredevil career in 1929. She broke countless bones, fractured her pelvis, and became shorter because of crushed vertebrae, but like Captain Frakes, she died of natural causes at an advanced age.

Another one of Mike's highlight acts, one that was especially popular at the Alabama State Fair, was Miss Victory, Victoria Zacchini, "The Cannonball Girl." The 22 year-old Victoria would be shot out of a cannon and land over 300 feet away in a large safety net. Her father, who invented the cannon shoot, explained that he broke his neck three times while perfecting the cannon in its early days in Cairo, Egypt. Victoria replaced her brother who went into the Navy. "I just take care always to land on my back," she would say nonchalantly. The Zacchini Family became famous for their cannonball act and played for circuses into the 1960s.

Mike also conducted rodeos, which were especially popular at the Texas State Fair in Dallas. Mike staged a world's championship rodeo contest there in 1931, with purses approximating

Victoria Zacchini, The Cannonball Girl

$15,000 given to the winners, a not inconsiderable sum during the Depression. (There were a number of rodeos claiming to be the world's championship in those days.) Some of the other locales Mike conducted rodeos included Chicago, Louisville, Shreveport, Toronto, Detroit, and Little Rock.

During one rodeo in Dallas in 1933, a local newspaper reported, "Four steers were said to be at large Monday night following their reported escape from their pens just before the night rodeo. Several cowboys sent in search of them failed to find any trace of the animals." It is unknown whether the steers were ever recovered.

As radio became more popular, Mike booked acts from the local Chicago WLS Barn Dance Troupe. WLS was one of the most popular radio stations in the country and because of its 50,000-watt, clear channel, one of the most widely heard during the evening. Its call letters stood for World's Largest Store, because it was originally owned by Sears Roebuck. The listenership extended across the Midwestern rural plains and as far north as Canada.

The Barn Dance started in 1924, and through the 1930s and 1940s ranked as America's most popular country music radio show, along with the legendary Grand Ole Opry. In 1932, it was renamed *The National Barn Dance*, when the NBC Blue Network broadcast a segment nationally. Stars included popular country music stars such as Gene Autry, Red Foley, and Homer and Jethro. (At the time country music was better known as "country and western" or "hillbilly" music. The Barn Dance remained on WLS through 1959, when the radio station was sold to ABC. The Barn Dance moved to one of Chicago's other big stations, WGN, until 1969. The call letters for WGN stood for World's Greatest Newspaper because it was owned by *The Chicago Tribune*. Ironically, WLS converted to a rock-and-roll format music in 1960 and became one of the country's top rock stations for twenty-five years.)

With his home base in Chicago, Mike was familiar with the Barn Dance performers, and one of the most popular ones that he booked was Patsy Montana, the first female country artist to have a million-selling single ("I Want To Be A Cowboy Sweetheart") and a member of the Country Music Hall of Fame. Rex Allen was another of his performers for a brief period of time. Rex was a cowboy singer, who later became a top-ten recording artist and cowboy star at Republic Pictures, the home studio of Gene Autry and Roy Rogers. Rex's movie work at Republic eventually earned him a star on the Hollywood Walk of Fame. (In those days, every

Patsy Montana

Rex Allen

good cowboy needed a sidekick and his included Buddy Ebsen and Slim Pickens, both of whom went on to stardom themselves in movies and television. Buddy Ebsen became famous as Jed Clampett in the iconic 1960s sitcom, The *Beverly Hillbillies*. Slim Pickens rode an atomic bomb as it was dropped from a bomber in the classic 1964 movie, *Dr. Strangelove*.)

CHAPTER EIGHTEEN

A Painstaking Man
and Mud Opera Maestro

DURING A SUCCESSFUL OKLAHOMA STATE FAIR, *THE DAILY Oklahoman* once said of Mike Barnes that for nearly thirty years he was "virtually without competition in the field of booking hippodrome, stage and circus acts." What characteristics put him at the pinnacle of the profession? Certainly his eye for talent, his deal-making skills, his willingness to take risks, and his ability to read an audience. But as much as any of those things it was his attention to detail. When planning a fair, he left nothing to chance. And as the first major fair booking agent to go into producing, he put months, sometimes years, into perfecting the acts he put on for the public.

At every major production, it seemed Mike was everywhere. One moment he was in the stands watching the performance, the next minute he would be backstage checking the lighting, the sound or the running time of the performance. Soon he would be back in the stands with the customers. (And you could almost trace his trail by the ubiquitous chewed toothpicks he would leave all over the fairgrounds.) When it rained heavily, as it often did in the Midwest during the summer, he called his big productions "mud operas," and he was fond of saying, "These mud operas are not as simple to run as they look." (*The Daily Oklahoman* called him "The Mud Opera Maestro.")

There was nothing Mike did not attend to. In the morning, he would crawl under the stage to ensure it was sturdy enough for the elephant acts. Then it was on to the dressing rooms before a check of the lighting and sound systems. Woe to the electrician he once caught napping instead of checking the lighting. Mike said, "That guy went to sleep on me, but he won't do that again."

When he assumed production responsibilities, Mike was even more meticulous. He spent five years perfecting his star production, "World on Parade." He told an interviewer, "Every bit of the show has been thought out for months. All the music was especially adapted for our use. The costumes were designed for the show and all scenery was constructed to fit the needs of this one performance. The members of the cast are most interesting, some coming from Europe for this show alone. I wish the audience could know them personally."

He had to audition 300 chorus girls for only sixteen roles. When the sixteen were selected, their chorus line performance was so good in rehearsal that a representative of the Schubert Theater signed them to work on Broadway during the winter. Mike took pride in the fact that he rarely had to cut an act after the show went on the road for its first public test.

We are far removed from the state fairs of the 1920s through the 1950s that Mike Barnes was so instrumental in providing with talent and producing. However, an article he kept in his scrapbook from 1925 entitled "It's Good Enough" by Dr. Frank

MUD OPERA Maestro

THAT inconspicuous little guy, with the gray hair, gray suit, and gray-blue eyes flitting around the night grandstand show of the Oklahoma State Fair every year—for years and years—is M. H. Barnes, Chicago, one of the biggest names in show business.

The calendar says he's 72-years-old. He's virtually retired. But watch him go! First he's in the stands to listen and watch. Then backstage to yell at someone about lighting, sound, or time. Then back in the stands he goes.

There's been only one change through the years. He's virtually quit breaking toothpicks. In the old days he could be trailed with little pieces of wood all over the place—particularly on opening night. But he still worries and frets, while the old hands who know and love him, watch and grin.

After all, this show went on the road without him. It's the first one in years. But when summer began to wane, and the leaves up north began to turn a bit, well it was fair time again, and like an old fire horse, he had to come back to the fire.

The Barnes story recently was called "from rags to riches," in a close-up written for The Billboard, national amusement weekly. It certainly is as American as they come, a story of a newsboy, who's grown into a big shot.

It's a long-way from the 10-year-old boy who ran away from home to New York, sold newspapers on the streets, and lived in coal boxes to the Mr. Barnes of Chicago, large scale real estate operator, trader on the commodity and stock markets, and owner of one of the most valuable stamp collections in the country.

Mike was hungry in those days. He sold papers from Park Row down through Chinatown to Houston street. When he decided that "there ought to be an easier way to make a living," he took a job as a cabin boy and shipped out on a Panama-bound freighter. The old sailing ship ran out of favorable winds—and it was a case of fish to eat. That was rough, too.

When Mike Barnes got back to Galveston, finally, he went back to New York, sold papers and saved enough to buy a new suit, and went to work as a messenger boy on Wall Street. He had had only one year of public schooling when he ran away. Aware of his lack of education, he began going to night school, finally went to work for a German language newspaper.

He worked for a while as a printer's devil, then in the editorial department of the old New York World before going into the circulation department. He had been hungry. He learned to save money. He still does—and takes quite a bit of kidding about it. But he had saved enough by the time he was 20 to start building apartment-houses in New York. He made a fortune—and lost it in the panic of 1909.

This time he started as a salesman for a tobacco company, saved $50, and took a fling at speculating in cotton—and made the $11,000 which was his stake in show business.

But it wasn't all easy sailing. While

Mike Barnes . . . he's come a long way

he came to Chicago to join his brother in the theatrical booking business by buying a carnival. That taught him one thing more and that is "never monkey with a business proposition you know nothing about."

His second business principal seems to be that if you do know, then back your judgment to the limit, with all the brains and money at your command.

That's the reason night grandstand shows exist the way they do today. Barnes was coming down this direction, working for his brother. He and Ralph T. Hemphill, Oklahoma State fair manager, conceived the idea together that the loud speaker made a different kind of show possible.

They tried it on a small scale—and Barnes went back to Chicago to sell the idea to his brother. It was tough, but he is today regarded as the first big booking agent to go into the business of being a producer—and it's been far from an unprofitable venture with him.

Barnes sold shows, and took the

risks, during the agriculture depression of the 1930's, when no fair manager expected to make ends meet. He speculated in corn—both on the market and in the deals that he made with his friends all over the country to bring them shows that would help pay out their fairs.

Barnes' interests have broadened through the years. He has almost as many friends in Oklahoma City among bankers, stock and commodity brokers, and hotel men as among those who are interested in show business. In good weather he will be downtown.

But when the clouds begin to gather, and there may be trouble, or on opening night when things go wrong, if they're going to, you'll find "Mike" all over the place.

"After all," he grins, "these mud operas are not as simple to run as they look."

But go ahead and have fun watching the show. It's a cinch that he will be out there seeing that things go without a hitch.

"Mud Opera Maestro"

Crane published by the now defunct McClure Newspaper Syndicate gives us a clue to his mindset during those years:

> *When someone doing a piece of work says, "Let it go; that's good enough!" It is generally a pretty good sign it is not good enough. If it were, no one would need convincing. I think it was Ed Howe who said that most new things are largely old things done better by painstaking men. "Painstaking men" is a classification that fits most of those who have done big things and made great discoveries. Taking pains is a fairly good definition of that zenith of human efficiency called "genius." Probably the most prevalent weakness of the human animal is a lack of persistence; of seeing a job through to the end: of sticking at a piece of work until it is well done. In the struggle for advancement in the world two men often times have the same ability and fight along neck and neck for a time. The one who pulls ahead on the final homestretch under such conditions is almost always the one who has trained himself to take pains. A slovenly carelessness is the dragon everyone has to slay.*

Mike Barnes slayed the dragon of slovenly carelessness.

CHAPTER NINETEEN

The War and Beyond

IT WASN'T LONG AFTER THE AMERICAN ECONOMY BEGAN improving and the Depression ended that the country was thrust into another national emergency—World War II. (Some historians posit that the United States did not actually come out of the Depression until it entered the war after the Japanese attack on Pearl Harbor in 1941. These historians claim the country did not emerge out of economic stagnation until wartime production geared up.) While America mobilized for war, this presented a potential problem for the entertainment industry in general, and state fairs specifically.

In fact, America at war was starved for entertainment; many state fairs broke attendance records during the war. (Hollywood also enjoyed booming attendance and profits from 1942–1946.) But the state fair audiences were different from the prewar crowds; there were fewer draft-age men, more women and children. Mike had to reconfigure the acts to appeal to the new demographic of his crowd—more child-friendly acts, circus and rodeo acts, and light operas. In addition, many of the performers he employed from Europe were unavailable because of the war.

Ace Lilliard and His Circus of Death

Because Capt. Frakes was in the Army and Lillian Boyer was retired, Mike needed daredevil acts. He frequently employed pole sitters, and men and women who were human cannonballs. They were shot out of a cannon and would land in a net hundreds of feet away. (In the event of high winds, the act would have to be cancelled because too many performers were blown beyond the safety netting.)

For his feature daredevil in the late 1930s and early 1940s, Mike chose Ace Lilliard, a former rodeo cowboy who transitioned into daring automobile stunts. The bill often read "Ace Lilliard's Circus of Death," featuring Ace Lilliard jumping a gap of death as he jumps his car 40 feet high." One of Ace's favorite stunts was standing on his head on the hood of a car traveling 30 miles per hour. He would routinely drive a sedan through a flaming tunnel of fire at 35 miles per hour. Ace also liked to speed his car up a ramp, sail over two buses and a pair of automobiles spanning 80 feet of space, land on a wrecked car, and bounce to earth. (In the spirit of full disclosure he was strapped in, wearing a football helmet.)

As the course of the war was turning toward the Allies in 1943 and 1944, Mike would put on the type of patriotic act that he always tried to include in his shows. His "Wings of Freedom" show at the Akron Rubber Bowl in 1944 featured comedians, acrobats, a magician, a dog act, an electric guitarist who could make his guitar talk (Bert Lynn, an important figure in the development of the electric guitar), dancers, singers, a 205-foot high pole act, and Miss Victory being shot out of a cannon. Thirty-two chorus girls did a stirring patriotic finale. At the war's end, the act was enhanced with other performers and called "Allies Victorious," and it became especially popular with crowds everywhere.

Ironically, one of the biggest problems with performances Mike put on during the war was that he had to scale back his legendary fireworks finale, because of wartime restrictions on the use of sulfur and magnesium, key ingredients in fireworks.

After the 1945 fair season, Mike planned on retiring. He had been in fair booking and grandstand production for 35 years, and he sold his interest in the Barnes-Carruthers Theatrical Enterprise to Sam Levy and associates. Levy had joined Fred and Mike in 1923, and he had been a de facto partner since Ed Carruthers died in 1935. In a formal statement Mike mailed to Levy and his business associates, he explained that, "piloting the business of Barnes-Carruthers thru the grueling war and Depression periods has been a severe strain on my health. Although a prosperous era is ahead of us, I nevertheless, under strict advice

Billie in St. Petersburg in 1946

of my physicians, find that I must take a long needed rest . . . I hope that a few months' rest will make it possible for me to visit the circuits next fall. I owe it to my family to retire from active business at this time."

He had been devoting more time to his family during the war years; there was less traveling as his daughters grew into young women. Mike believed that his daughters should both attend college, a progressive notion at the time. During the war, his older daughter, B.J., attended Barat College in Lake Forest, Illinois. His younger daughter, Mary, attended Northwestern University in Evanston, Illinois. Mary recalled Mike helping her with college term papers. That someone who had only a year of formal education and several years of night schooling could help his daughter at one of the nation's top universities is truly extraordinary. It is a testimony to the education he got outside of school.

After selling his interest in Barnes-Carruthers, Mike took his family down to St. Petersburg, Florida, where he planned to rest. But before leaving for Florida, he gave an indication he was not done with the fair business. He told associates he would volunteer the benefit of his experience to the organization in an advisory capacity. He maintained he would always continue to have the interests of the fair business at heart.

And he would be true to his word. Between his family, the fair business, and his other interests, Mike did not really retire after World War II.

Chapter Twenty

Retirement After the War

No sooner than Mike announced his retirement, he was back in the game. While his loyal employees now owned the business that they helped Mike create, he went to about five fair shows every year in an advisory capacity. These fairs, the biggest and most popular, had the Barnes-Carruthers "A-list" acts (at this point the firm was booking at least 300 acts per year). His experience proved invaluable and his reputation was instrumental in helping those fairs become even more prosperous.

After the business was sold in 1946, the fairs that Mike loved to visit most were also the ones he had the longest and fondest attachments to, especially the Oklahoma State Fair and the Kansas State Fair. When he came to the Oklahoma State Fair in 1948, *The Daily Oklahoman* did a profile of him that began,

> *That inconspicuous little guy, with the gray hair, gray suit, and gray-blue eyes flitting around the grandstand of the Oklahoma State Fair every year—for years and years—is M. H. Barnes, Chicago, one of the biggest names in show business.*

The calendar says he's 72 years old. He's virtually retired. But watch him go! . . . There's been only one change through the years. He's virtually quit breaking toothpicks. In the old days he could be trailed with little pieces of wood all over the place—particularly on opening nights. But he still worries and frets, while the old hands who know him and love him, watch and grin.

After all, the show went on the road without him. It's the first one in years. But when the summer began to wane, and the leaves up north began to turn a bit, well it was fair time and again, and like an old fire horse, he had to come back to the fire.

Mike continued to advise to the Oklahoma State Fair into the 1950s. Each year in the early 1950s, the fair's attendance records were broken; by 1954, nearly 400,000 people attended.

During the 1950s, he also supervised at the Kansas State Fair in Hutchinson to great acclaim (*"Mike Barnes has done it again"*). He felt that for years his people were treated better there than in almost any other venue. He believed the Kansas Fairgrounds were laid out better than anywhere else, and the stagehands were among the best. He attended the Hutchinson Fair for over 40 consecutive years. In his 70s he said, "I'll keep coming back to Hutchinson as long as my welcome holds out."

At one show in the early 1950s at the Kansas Fair, though, Mike was confronted by a situation he had never faced before. In the middle of an evening performance, a fierce wind blew into the fairgrounds. Mike was inspecting the floodlights and revue show scenery, which was threatening to blow away. At that moment, his aerial artist, Betty Fox, began climbing the 125-foot pole with only an 18-inch platform at the top. Fearful of the winds, he ordered her to stop and come down. "Then I got busy somewhere else and the next thing I saw, there she was, up on top."

While some stagehands tried furiously to save the scenery, others were yelling up to her, "Come down Betty, for God's sakes, come down." It was to no avail as Betty went on with her act far above the grandstand, amidst the swirling winds.

Mike recalled, "We were afraid lightning would hit her or the wind would blow her off the pedestal. I've honestly never seen anything like it in fifty years of show business." Even with this, at the end of the fair, officials once again congratulated Mike for a job well done and for all the hard work he had put in. And this was years after he had "retired"!

He also continued his love-hate relationship with his old friend Maurice Jencks at the Topeka Free Fair into the 1950s. As *The Topeka State Journal* reported in 1950, "Mike Barnes of Chicago, owner of the famous night shows that play the Kansas Free Fair each year, was a visitor to Topeka one day this week, scheduled to become engaged in the yearly handwaving, pencil-sharpening, and voice-raising controversy with Maurice Jencks over the next fair night show contract. But this week, Mike called a truce. 'I have a new grandson,' (his daughter Mary's son, Christopher) he told Maurice. Let's talk about him instead of the show contract. Oh, yes, and I have another grandchild due in May (B.J.'s daughter, Betsy).'"

'Mike,' Maurice said, 'I had a granddaughter nine years ago but I can't remember that the event brought a tenth of one percent advantage to me that year. I offer my congratulations to you and Mrs. Barnes and your entire family—here's how—but let me tell you something—the Kansas Free Fair next September wants that night show on a percentage basis, you get—.

The battle was on!"

Two years later, *The Journal* covered what may have been their last meeting,

"Mike and Maurice now look back on the years with high good humor. 'I guess we are getting mellow in our old age', Mike says."

CHAPTER TWENTY-ONE

Another Skill: Investing

IN RETIREMENT, MIKE GOT A CHANCE TO SHOW THAT HE WAS a shrewd appraiser of things other than fair talent. Whether it was stocks, commodities, or real estate, he had a keen eye for value. Even after he retired, he maintained his habit of rising at 6:00 a.m., having breakfast at 7:00 a.m., talking to his financial advisors, and then checking his investments and real estate holdings—most of which were quite successful. In a review of the 1946 Topeka Free Fair, one of the first Mike attended as a fair consultant after his retirement, this item was buried in *The Topeka State Journal*:

> *Mike Barnes, millionaire owner of the night shows at the Free Fair, grabbed a State Journal Tuesday evening as soon as he could find a newsboy. Did he turn to the review of his show? No! He dived inside for the New York stock market quotations.*

Mike, of course, had experience with the New York Stock Exchange as a messenger on Wall Street when he was a boy a half century earlier, and he eventually became a member of the Exchange. He referred to it as a "hedging operation."

He was also a member of the Chicago Board of Trade. The Chicago Board of Trade (CBOT) was established in 1848 as a commodity exchange. It started with 82 members, but most of Chicago's early grain traders traded wheat and oats on the city streets. Early experience was not promising. On four days in July 1851, only one member showed up, and no one showed up on four other days—not even the free lunch offered could increase attendance.

The situation changed during the Crimean War in the mid-1850s. Grain from Europe became scarce, increasing demand for American grain. With wheat shipments rising in volume significantly and going through Chicago, it became more efficient for grain brokers to do their buying and selling in a central location, the Board of Trade. Soon, the CBOT became an important financial institution internationally, with significant influence on the grain trade worldwide.

In 1856, the board established a grading system, creating standards for the quality of commodities. Traders could now buy a quantity of a specific grade of wheat, rather than just buying or selling sacks of wheat. Eventually, this made it possible to buy and sell contracts for delivery of grain in the future. This "futures trading" exploded after the Civil War.

The Chicago Tribune reported that by 1875, the year before Mike Barnes was born, the sale of grain futures was $2 billion, while the actual grain trade itself was only one tenth of that. Eventually, through an open outcry system (that is now essentially gone due to computers) futures in all types of agricultural contracts and financial instruments became a vital part of the CBOT. It is unknown what Mike paid for his seat on the CBOT, likely no more than a couple of thousand dollars. By 2002, the price of a seat had peaked at $2.6 million, although it has dropped significantly since then to several hundred thousand dollars.

Mike learned about commodity trading early on—his first big stake in show business was the $11,000 he made in cotton futures in New York after the Panic of 1907 (even though he lost that on his first carnival venture). With nearly forty years of experience traveling the Midwest on the fair circuit, talking with farmers and other businessmen, Mike had unrivaled access to what was happening on the farms. He could find out firsthand from the farmers themselves whether it would be a boom or bust year for many of their crops. This knowledge of the agricultural markets would be invaluable to him when he returned to Chicago. With his knowledge of the markets, Mike became as respected on LaSalle Street, the financial center of Chicago, as he had been on Clark Street, where he appraised talent. Moreover, he often used his speculation skills to help finance fair shows like the one in Iowa, where the fair managers were concerned they could not make ends meet.

Had he not gone into the booking business, Mike likely would have amassed a large fortune in real estate. Once more, he started out young, buying buildings in New York City, but he got his real experience when he came to Chicago by working for brother Fred and managing his real estate holdings. After Fred's death in 1929, Mike continued to manage some of those holdings, which included some of the most valuable real estate in the Chicago Loop. His transactions consistently turned a profit, and one of his most impressive deals was the 1956 purchase and renovation of a new home for the Showmen's League of America at the prestigious Loop intersection of Franklin and Randolph Streets.

As *The Chicago Sun-Times* reported, "Mike Barnes, long known for his keen knowledge of property values in Downtown Chicago had first learned of the building's availability, and had reported it to a committee headed by Rudy Singer, which had been named to determine possible new locations for the club's quarters." Mike later helped finance the modernization of the building's interior and exterior by purchasing debentures personally.

Mike might have had an extremely successful career in investments or real estate. With his acumen, he might have become one of the country's richest men, but America, without having him for state fairs, would have been poorer for it.

CHAPTER TWENTY-TWO

Charity

Freely have you received; freely give.
—MATTHEW 10:8

THROUGHOUT HIS LIFE, MIKE NEVER NEGLECTED TO INCLUDE giving freely to others as part of his personal story; charity was part of his nature. In 1927, he donated to the relief effort in Louisiana after The Great Mississippi Flood of 1927. Barnes-Carruthers furnished the Louisiana State Fair with outdoor show attractions, and when the Mississippi River remained above flood stage for 153 days, leaving 10,000 square miles in 20 parishes underwater, Mike sent a check to the State Fair Association.

The Times-Picayune, in a story headlined "Chicago Man Gives Cash To Relief," described the conditions,

The need for funds with which to carry on the rehabilitation work in flooded sectors is growing more urgent daily as the farmers get back to the homes from which they fled when threatened by high waters. The small farmers and negro

The Great Mississippi Flood of 1927

tenants will have hard sledding this summer if enough money is not forthcoming for rehabilitation work. The Red Cross will endeavor to take care of those people who would otherwise actually be without food if such aid was not given.

The Flood of 1927 was called "the greatest peace-time calamity in the history of the country" by Secretary of Commerce Herbert Hoover. Later, during the Depression, Barnes-Carruthers helped out smaller towns hit by lesser disasters such as storm-related damage, time and again. It naturally generated goodwill, which was beneficial to business, but Mike took a personal interest in helping out, which was demonstrated through his private donations.

He donated generously to both Catholic and Jewish charities, often anonymously. From his time in Nebraska, he came to know Father Flanagan, founder of Boys Town. Father Edward Flanagan was born in Ireland and came to the United States in 1904. After being ordained, he was assigned to the Diocese of Omaha, Nebraska. For several years, he worked with the homeless of Omaha, but eventually his primary interest became children and families. As a social reformer and spokesman for children, Father Flanagan believed that children had the right to be valued, the right to the basic necessities of life, and the right to be protected. He fought to close reformatories and juvenile facilities where children were imprisoned and abused. In 1917, Father Flanagan opened Father Flanagan's Boys' Home, which became popularly known as Boys Town. Boys Town offered a fresh start to every boy, regardless of race, creed or religious denomination. It accepted any boy, including those who were in prison for serious crimes, and it paid especial attention to the most disadvantaged. (The story of Boys Town is told in the 1938 movie *Boys Town* starring Mickey Rooney and Spencer Tracy, who won an Academy Award as Father Flanagan.)

In Mike's scrapbook, there is an endearing photo of Father Flanagan with a young boy and a dog as they fish off a pier. When Mike died among the donations in his will was $1000 to Father Flanagan's Boys Town, in Boys Town, Douglas County Nebraska.

One of the things Mike often did in retirement was scan *The Chicago Tribune* for tales of misfortune that had befallen children. One such 1955 article entitled, "Shirley's Plea Is Santa's Cue— Gifts Galore Replace Stolen Ones."

Generous Chicagoans assured a 12 year-old Michigan girl yesterday that the Christmas stockings of her five brothers and sisters would be filled with duplicates of the presents she selected for them last weekend on a Chicago shopping trip.

They answered the appeal of Shirley Benjamin of Route 1 Watervliet, who wrote to "Dear Mr. Editor" at The Tribune to tell how the gifts she had bought with the money she

Father Flanagan. COURTESY OF BOYS TOWN

earned picking berries and tomatoes last summer had been stolen Saturday night from the family car.

"We only spent $15," she wrote. "It was not much, but it was all we had to make a nice Christmas for the six kids in our family. Maybe if the burglar would read this letter he would send them back to us or to the police station where we reported it, The Town Hall station on Addison and Halsted. The burglar may not have read Shirley's letter but a 78 year-old grandfather of six did . . . Shirley found a Santa in Michael H. Barnes of 819 Junior Terrace, the 78 year-old grandfather. When Barnes read Shirley's letter in The Tribune, he telephoned Sgt. John Glas of the Town Hall station. Glas told Barnes Shirley had returned home so Barnes sent Shirley a check for $15.

Chapter Twenty-Three

Hobbies

For one as busy as Mike was with fair business ten to twelve months per year, it might be logical to assume he had little spare time to do much else. In fact, he had several hobbies, which he cultivated assiduously. Mike liked to play cards, gin rummy especially, and with his mental acuity he was an expert gin rummy player. (To master gin rummy requires a good memory, an understanding of your opponent's strategy and style of play, and a willingness to make calculated gambles—all skills Mike excelled at.)

He enjoyed theater and the opera and included both in many of his shows (the sophisticated shows he transferred to the fairgrounds as the "Mud Opera Maestro" were not invariably popular with the fair crowd, and he would occasionally have to tailor the shows to his audiences' tastes.) He had an unusual musical talent: because he listened to so much music, he could play by ear. He would hear a tune once and be able to play it on the piano. (According to his granddaughter Gail, one reason Mike ran away when he was a boy was because his stepmother would not let him play the piano at home.) But Mike had two hobbies he loved more than any others—stamp collecting and anything associated with the water.

From an early age, Mike was a stamp collector, and over the years he accumulated quite a valuable collection. Stamp collecting began with the original postage stamp, a picture of Queen Victoria known as the Penny Black, issued in Great Britain in 1840. Once many countries began issuing postage stamps en masse, stamp collecting became a legitimate hobby. By the 1860s, stamp collectors had sprung up in Europe, Great Britain, and their respective colonies. Americans, including children and teenagers, became avid stamp collectors in the later decades of the nineteenth century. In our computer/email age when stamp collecting has fallen out of favor, it is hard to imagine how popular a hobby it once was. In fact, some adults amassed collections that became quite valuable; an especially rare stamp could fetch thousands of dollars. Today some stamps have sold for over $1 million.

In a 1952 interview with *The Topeka State Journal*, Mike described how he first got interested in stamp collecting. It came about at the turn of the century when he served as a broker in the sale of a valuable stamp collection while he was a copy boy on *The New York Journal*. It provided him with some of his first real money.

He recalled, "One of the editors of foreign news was an Austrian, who lived over in Brooklyn. He got sick and worked at home, so I used to go over and pick up his copy at his house. When he died, he left his widow practically nothing except a stamp collection. I told her I'd try and sell it for her. She wanted $150 for it.

One of the men at the office offered to buy a few of the stamps for ten cents apiece, but I took the collection down to Nassau Street where the stamp dealers were located. A dealer asked me how much. I didn't want to put a price on it, so I asked him what he would give. When he said $300, I tried to act like I wasn't surprised and told him I had to have $450 or nothing. I started to walk out a couple of times, but we finally made a deal for $400. I gave all the money to the widow in Brooklyn, she gave me $100, and that was the first big money I ever made . . . it was really big money in those days—about like a thousand dollars today."

That experience not only provided Mike with his first big money, it gave him an interest in collecting stamps himself. Over the next decades, through his frequent travels, including to Europe to evaluate fair talent, and with his contacts with other collectors and dealers, he was able to create an impressive stamp collection.

He also loved the water—especially swimming, sailing, and fishing. At 5'8" and 150 pounds he was thin, lithe, and muscular even in his later years. He had the ideal body for a swimmer and gave swimming lessons when he was young.

(He also helped train "physical culture" classes. Physical culture was a health and strength training movement that was developed in Germany in the mid-nineteenth century. German immigrants brought the movement to the United States, and it was especially popular in the German neighborhoods of big cities like New York and Chicago. Not unlike today's physical fitness trends, physical culture emphasized exercise through gymnastics and contact sports like wrestling and boxing, as well as using weights and medicine balls.)

Mike continued to swim to stay in shape throughout his life. (Just as it is interesting to wonder whether Mike came into contact with Charlie Chaplin and Gloria Swanson in their early days in Chicago, it is tempting to speculate whether he knew another German immigrant to the North Side of Chicago with an interest in swimming, who was a lifeguard at the Oak Street Beach—Johnny Weissmuller, who played Tarzan in the movies.)

Fishing was another one of Mike's favorite pastimes. It was often difficult for him to break away during the fair season to go fishing in the Midwest, but occasionally he and Billie could get some fishing in during the Louisiana State Fair in Shreveport, where Billie had relatives. Mike, Billie, and the two girls would spend time in the winter in St. Petersburg and Miami Beach, where the fishing was always good. Mike's scrapbook is loaded with pictures of the family displaying impressive strings of large fish they caught. (There is also a nice one of Mike proudly holding his fishing rod.)

Later in life, when Mike had more spare time in Chicago with his family, they were able to fish in Lake Michigan from their cabin cruiser leaving from Montrose Harbor, only a few blocks from the family home on Junior Terrace. They belonged to the new Corinthian Yacht Club in Montrose Harbor. (The Chicago Corinthian Yacht Club was founded in 1934, when the schooner *Gaviota* sailed into the Harbor. The *Gaviota* had been built for Franklin Delano Roosevelt, an avid seaman, and at the request of the Chicago Park District, the owners of the *Gaviota* transferred their mooring from the overcrowded Belmont Harbor to the new empty harbor facility at the eastern end of Montrose Avenue.)

The man who once nervously chewed up toothpicks on the fairgrounds supervising every aspect of his acts, would kick back and relax when he got a chance to sail. Besides the boats the Barnes family owned in Chicago, they also owned boats

Billie with her catch

Mike relaxing with his fishing rod

Corinthian Yacht Club c. 1940

in Florida. Mike used to say, "Boating was much cheaper than night clubbing."

In Florida, they would sail in Tampa Bay and out into the Gulf of Mexico on their sailboat, the *Athanasia*. In the 1930s, they owned a cabin cruiser in Chicago, the *Jimmy Jay*. When daughters B.J. and Mary were young, the family would take it out on the lake. (The *Jimmy Jay* is the family boat where a young Mary tried varnish the teakwood.) After Mike retired, the *Jimmy Jay* was replaced by the *Billie Gail* (named after Mike's wife and first grandchild), anchored in Belmont Harbor, a little farther south. With his granddaughter Gail by his side, Mike would rev up the Billie Gail for a turn past the Chicago skyline. Afterwards, Gail would fall asleep below deck in her cabin.

The purchase of the *Billie Gail* proved to be quite an adventure. Mike went with his crew to Holland, Michigan, to pick up the 41-foot Chris Craft and cross Lake Michigan to Chicago.

Billie and granddaughter Gail on the cabin cruiser named after them

Two hours out of Holland, the ship ran into a nor'easter and huge waves enveloped the boat. The ship-to-shore telephone stopped working and the water pumps failed. Mike and the crew took turns pumping water by hand, and the captain attempted to steer the boat on course to Chicago. The captain finally got the boat on course as they steered toward Belmont Harbor. There was only one problem. Mike noticed a forest of tall trees along the coastline. "This isn't Chicago," Mike told the captain. "Our first view

The Billie Gail

of factory chimneys was familiar all right, but there's no forest close to the industrial area of the Chicago lakeshore."

When they hailed a Coast Guard cruiser and exchanged megaphone conversations, they discovered they were just outside of Milwaukee, 95 miles north of Chicago. They tied up overnight, had the pumps repaired and set out for Chicago the next morning. They were hit by another storm and tried to get into the nearest harbor at the Wisconsin-Illinois border. Unfortunately, the harbor was equipped only for sailboats, not cruisers, and they ran aground as they tried to exit the harbor.

Mike later recalled, "In the next 24 hours, I would have sold that boat for 50 cents on the dollar. But when we finally got home and realized what a beating she had taken in that fierce storm, we figured she was too seaworthy to abandon."

Chapter Twenty-Four

Family

For many years, Mike was essentially on the road for up to ten months, supervising fairs from April through October, and for another three months auditioning performers, traveling across the country or to Europe seeking new acts and talent, or negotiating fair contracts for the upcoming year. But his surviving daughter, Mary, and his grandchildren who knew him before he died, all described him as a model husband and father.

Because he was gone so much, Mike tried to spend as much time as possible with his family when he was home. Although the school year conflicted with some of the fairs, he occasionally brought the family to the fairs when he was working. Billie accompanied him to the Louisiana State Fair in Shreveport, where she enjoyed the fishing. While the girls were out of school in August, Mike would bring them to the Ionia Free Fair in Michigan, where the circus was one of the major attractions. B.J. and Mary would enjoy posing with and riding on the elephants, who were available between grandstand acts. They would also enjoy the parade and the automobile races at Ionia.

B.J., Judy the elephant, Mary, and cousin Beatrice at the Ionia Fair

Mike at the automobile races

Mike was an aficionado of automobile racing as far back as the 1910s, and this no doubt had a part in him hiring automobile daredevil Ace Lilliard and his "Circus of Death" for so many of his fair shows.

One of their favorite trips as a family was to Albuquerque, New Mexico. Billie, an accomplished equestrian, often rode with the local Native American horsemen, and the family became

Mike and Billie

Billie and Native American Horsemen in New Mexico

quite close with many of the village tribe. While not the horse-woman their mother was, both girls became expert riders. The girls also took flying and music lessons.

The family also travelled to Hot Springs, Arkansas, a favorite getaway for the famous and the notorious in the 1940s, where they enjoyed the therapeutic thermal waters. Another Barnes destination was Colorado; the family stayed at the Brook Forest Inn outside Denver. The historic Brook Forest Inn was built in 1909 in a Victorian Style and was said to be haunted. From there the family visited Pike's Peak, 90 miles away.

Back in Chicago, the Barnes home at 819 Junior Terrace was welcoming and friendly. The girls belonged to the "Junior Terrace Gang," a group of neighborhood kids who often congregated at the Barnes house (they were all friendly neighbors and bore

Brook Forest Inn, Colorado

On Vacation, Visiting Pikes Peak

no resemblance to the vicious gangs Mike grew up with at the turn of the century on the Lower East Side). There were plenty of pets, including a series of dogs, and Christmas was always special. When the girls went off to college in the early 1940s, it gave Mike and Billie some time alone. Mike took a keen interest in the girls' studies and was a proud father at their graduations from college.

B.J. went on to marry one of Chicago's top general surgeons and had three children (Betsy, Pam, and Philip). Mary married the son of the founder of Motorola, one of America's most successful corporations. (Mike consented to both marriages with the proviso that both girls finish college, which they did.)

Christmas 1945

Mike and Mary on her wedding day. COURTESY OF STUART-RODGERS PHOTOGRAPHY

Mary and her husband, Bob Galvin. COURTESY OF STUART-RODGERS PHOTOGRAPHY

Mike, Billie, Bob's father Paul, and Bob's Aunt Rose. COURTESY OF STUART-RODGERS PHOTOGRAPHY

Mike and B.J. on her wedding day. COURTESY OF STUART-RODGERS PHOTOGRAPHY

B.J. with her husband Phil and Billie. COURTESY OF STUART-RODGERS PHOTOGRAPHY

Wives Mary and B.J. with husbands Phil and Bob. COURTESY OF STUART-RODGERS PHOTOGRAPHY

Mike had an excellent relationships with both of his sons-in-law. He would occasionally visit Bob, Mary's husband, and the two would go into the den for long conversations. Mike and Billie also got along very well with Bob's father, Paul.

Mary had four children (Gail, Dawn, Chris, and Mike). Her first child, Gail Annette, was Mike's first grandchild. Mary's younger son was named after him. Mike was fortunate to live long enough to see the birth of six of his seven grandchildren. He died before the birth of his youngest grandchild, B.J.'s son, Philip.

Because Mike married later in life, most of his grandchildren have few personal recollections of him. Three of the grandchildren, Gail, Dawn, and Mike, were able to remember at least a little about him, more than sixty years later.

From Gail Galvin Ellis, Mike's first grandchild:

I have amazing memories about my grandfather, even though I was only a little girl. My memories are from when I was about four, five, six or seven (Mike died when Gail was eight.) He was my favorite relative, and we had a unique relationship. He treated me like I walked on water.

I was the first grandchild in the family, and because I was a girl and my grandfather had two daughters, I think he was used to girls. He was comfortable with them. He'd taking me riding in a big gray car, and I'd sit in the backseat with a lap robe to keep my legs warm. He had some real estate holdings, and each month he would go around to collect the rents. No one else liked to go with him, but I loved it. I would get all dressed up in leggings and a matching coat, and when we would ride around the neighborhood, I felt like a princess. I think my favorite place to go in the car with him was the zoo. He loved to go to the zoo, and so did I. We would go to the Lincoln Park Zoo, where they had a gorilla named Bushman. (Bushman was arguably the most famous gorilla in the world. He was brought to Chicago from Cameroon in 1930, and he was seen by tens of millions of people at the Lincoln Park Zoo from 1930 until his death in 1951. He grew to be 6'2" and nearly 600 pounds, and he would perform for the zoogoers by scampering in his cage, banging the glass that separated him, swinging on his tire—one of his many tires was from Adolf Hitler's Mercedes—and occasionally throwing poop at the glass. When he died, his remains were preserved by taxidermists, and he is located today at the Field Museum in Chicago, where he continues to be a popular attraction.) We both loved to go and see Bushman, and my grandfather would take me any time. He said I'm taking you to see "your gorilla." We would walk up to his cage, and Bushman would bang on the glass and try and scare us.

    Another thing we would do together is go to the circus. When I was young, I thought his only job was booking acts for the circus. He knew all the circus performers. He would take me back to the dressing rooms of the freakshow performers— the bearded lady, the tall men, and the others. He would talk with all of them and introduce me. They were such interesting people and so nice. I guess he taught me not to judge people by their appearance. It was so much fun meeting them, then I would sit on his lap and watch the circus. He would buy me popcorn and Coke, which we shared, and when I got back home, Mom wasn't always happy that I ate so much popcorn and drank so much Coke.

I remember he would come back from Europe after looking for acts, and he would bring back dolls and beer steins from Germany. One year, he actually brought back a small car for the family, like a Volkswagen except that it had gull-wing doors and only three wheels. It was a Messerschmitt, and he took me for rides in it. I don't know what happened to it.

Bushman at the Lincoln Park Zoo

I could talk to my grandfather about anything. He was kind, sympathetic, and a good listener. We had an amazing relationship."

From Michael Galvin, Mike's grandson who Michael was named after:

As the youngest Galvin, born on July 8, 1952, I have only a few, vague but real, personal recollections. I regret that beyond these recollections, I cannot be more informative given my vintage.

First, as a very young, but somewhat aware child, I recall feeling very comfortable sitting on Mike's lap and horsing around with him. I recall sensing his disarming and welcoming smile. His energetic spirit. And hearty laugh.

Second, I recall that Mike took me to the first circus I ever attended. (Every year, Ringling Brothers would hold a circus at the Chicago Stadium. Traffic would be stopped as the animals moved down Ogden Avenue and Madison Street to the Stadium. The Chicago Bulls and Blackhawks, who played there, would leave town and play road games for the two-week duration of the circus.)

I only got to go because I pleaded so desperately to be a part of this outing with the other, older kids at a time when my parents thought I was too young. As it turns out, my parents were essentially right. I was so overwhelmed by the loudness of the music, snap of the whips, crack of the guns, and audience cheers, that I was scared and cried in distress. It was the circus equivalent of an infant freaking out at the sight of Santa Claus. I further recall that when Mike sat me in his lap and put his arms around me, I was immediately consoled. But, then I fell asleep on his chest for the remainder of most of the circus performance. For me, this outing was a great, if albeit unconventional, success because of Mike.

Third, Mike had a very unusual car, a German Messerschmitt microcar. It was very uncommon. It had only three wheels. And had a lot of pep. Mike used to like to drive that car to our St. Joan of Arc neighborhood in Skokie. Because he knew there would always be lots of enthusiastic kids like me from the old neighborhood who would want to sit on his lap in it and feel like we were driving it around the community. It's where I learned how to hold it together while waiting one's turn in line. . . .

1955 Messerschmitt KR200 microcar

Fourth, I recall that when Dad/Bob (Robert Galvin, son of Paul Galvin who founded Motorola) used to talk about Mike, he did so with genuine respect. He used to say that Mike was every bit as innovative and entrepreneurial in his field (entertainment) as Paul and Motorola were in electronics. I also recall as a child sensing that Dad and Mike appeared to enjoy one another's company and senses of humor. But, I can't remember (or probably didn't understand) what they were talking about.

From Dawn Galvin Meiners, Mike's second grandchild:

I was very small when Mike died, only six or seven, so I don't have many memories. But one thing I remember vividly is every Christmas morning, Mike would come to our house, usually early, before breakfast. He wore a nice suit, and he would pat us all on the head and smile. He would come in and wouldn't stay that long, but he would make sure to play with all of us. You could tell he really loved the grandchildren, and I wish I could have gotten to know him better when I was older. I think we would have had a really good time together. It's funny, because I don't think I ever remember seeing him when he was not dressed in a fine suit. He was an elegant dresser, and he and my grandmother were quite a good-looking couple.

CHAPTER TWENTY-FIVE

Epilogue: A Life Well Lived

MIKE BARNES DIED OF CORONARY THROMBOSIS ON MAY 29, 1956, a little more than a month short of his 80th birthday. According to his obituary in *Billboard*, "Even in the immediately hours before death closed in on him, Mike was all business. Knowing the end was near, he gave detailed instructions to members of his family and his business associates on what he wished them to do after his death." Among the donations mentioned in his will were $5000 each to the National Jewish Hospital in Denver, Colorado; Jewish Charities of Chicago; Catholic Charities of Chicago; United Charities of Chicago; Loyola Medical School of Chicago and the Mount Sinai Medical Research of Chicago. He also donated $2000 to St. Mary's Church of the Lake in Chicago, and $1000 to the Salvation Army and Boys Club of Chicago. The combined charitable givings in his will amounted to nearly $40,000, which would be the equivalent of close to $400,000 in 2019. The bulk of his estate was left to his wife of 36 years and his two daughters for whom he provided trusts. He also provided trusts for his grandchildren, born and to come.

The American writer Cynthia Ozick once said, "A biography can read like a novel." This was never more true than in the life and times of Mike Barnes; his biography was a true rags to riches "Horatio Alger" story.

During one of his last visits to the Kansas State Fair, Mike was profiled by a staff writer of *The Topeka State Journal*, Gordon Martin. Martin wrote,

> *Mike Barnes is a fabulous character—and that might qualify as the understatement of the year. If you'd see Mike milling around in the fair crowd, which he doesn't do so much anymore, he might be the last man on the lot you'd pick for a well-off gent, because Mike doesn't go for the big showman's splash—personally, that is. He saves it for the stage show.*
>
> *But packed into his small 148-pound frame beneath a thatch of silvery hair and behind his bespectacled blue eyes is a treasure of show-biz savvy. For this is the man who started on the sidewalks of New York, first as a copyboy in a newspaper office, later dabbling in carnivals but getting out quick, and then going on to the booking agency and stage show business that has made him wealthy.*

Fitting words, but if anything, incomplete. Mike's story was about far more than becoming a successful businessman. It was about grit, determination, overcoming adversity, and getting an education on the mean streets of New York and Chicago, an education that ultimately allowed him to travel in the rarefied circles of Wall Street and LaSalle Street. It is about a man who embodied what Rudyard Kipling once wrote about: the common touch. Mike truly could "walk with the crowd and keep his virtue or walk with Kings nor lose that common touch." This was a man who helped provide a resting place for nameless individuals who died decades before in a tragic fire and frequently went with his family to visit their graves.

In his life, Mike knew a panoply of people—from stars to second bananas to spear carriers and all the backstage hands without whom the performances could not go on. He could converse comfortably with politicians, journalists, financial mavens and the guys who cleaned up after the elephants in the circus. He was a friend and supporter of Father Flanagan from Boys Town.

He lived through several depressions and always emerged bloodied but unbowed. In addition, during his life he saw America fight in four wars, and he remained a patriot throughout. He loved America and wanted his audiences to love it as well, which is why he always included patriotic numbers in his shows.

Mike loved the arts, high and low, but even more than show business, Mike's life was about charity—he was a respected, but often anonymous patron and donor. Most importantly, he was about family—a loving husband and a proud, doting father and grandfather.

Amidst all this, Mike Barnes left a spirit of goodwill wherever he went in his extensive travels. He was an important figure in the story of entertainment in America in the first half of the twentieth century and his legacy endures to this day. The number of people whose lives he touched and who he entertained is in the millions.

He lived such a life that his epitaph might have been written by William Shakespeare, "He acted from honesty and for general good. His life was gentle, and the elements mixed so well in him that Nature might stand up and say to all the world, *'This was a man.'*"